299361

KT-460-636

Praise for

IDEA TO *Invention*

"*Idea to Invention* shows you through examples that everyone can be an inventor by finding solutions to common problems that people experience daily. If you want to turn your passion into a business and find meaning in your life, this is the book for you."

—Dan Schawbel, *New York Times* bestselling author of *Promote Yourself* and *Me 2.0*

"This is a great read. *Idea to Invention* not only holds your hand through the invention process but really encourages you every step of the way. Patricia demystifies inventing in a way that is easy to follow yet rigorous enough to make you the inventor you always dreamed of being."

—Dr. Gordon Adomdza, PhD—Entrepreneurship & Innovation Professor, Northeastern University

"As enchanting as it is informative, Patricia's book will help you master the invention process and achieve success in a timely and cost-efficient way."

—Guy Kawasaki, former Chief Evangelist of Apple and author of *The Art of the Start*

"Patricia Nolan-Brown has nailed it! For anyone new to the world of inventing and launching new products, this is the perfect guidebook—with specific how-to advice and what pitfalls to avoid. In addition, it is impressively up to date on how to use social media. This is the book I will recommend to all the callers who have an invention idea but don't know what to do next."

—Robert Hausslein, President of the Inventors Association of New England

IDEA TO *Invention*

What You Need to Know to Cash In on Your Inspiration

Patricia Nolan-Brown

AMACOM

AMERICAN MANAGEMENT ASSOCIATION
NEW YORK · ATLANTA · BRUSSELS · CHICAGO · MEXICO CITY ·
SAN FRANCISCO · SHANGHAI · TOKYO · TORONTO · WASHINGTON, D. C.

Bulk discounts available. For details visit:
www.amacombooks.org/go/specialsales
Or contact special sales:
Phone: 800-250-5308
Email: specialsls@amanet.org
View all the AMACOM titles at: www.amacombooks.org
American Management Association: www.amanet.org

This publication is designed to provide accurate and authoritative information in regard to the subject matter covered. It is sold with the understanding that the publisher is not engaged in rendering legal, accounting, or other professional service. If legal advice or other expert assistance is required, the services of a competent professional person should be sought.

Library of Congress Cataloging-in-Publication Data

Nolan-Brown, Patricia.
 Idea to invention : what you need to know to cash in on your inspiration / Patricia Nolan-Brown.
 pages cm
 Includes bibliographical references and index.
 ISBN-13: 978-0-8144-3293-8
 ISBN-10: 0-8144-3293-X
 1. Inventions. 2. Creative thinking. 3. New products. I. Title.
 T212.N62 2014
 658.5'75—dc23
                                        2013027426

© 2014 Patricia Nolan-Brown.
All rights reserved.
Printed in the United States of America.

This publication may not be reproduced, stored in a retrieval system, or transmitted in whole or in part, in any form or by any means, electronic, mechanical, photocopying, recording, or otherwise, without the prior written permission of AMACOM, a division of American Management Association, 1601 Broadway, New York, NY 10019

The scanning, uploading, or distribution of this book via the Internet or any other means without the express permission of the publisher is illegal and punishable by law. Please purchase only authorized electronic editions of this work and do not participate in or encourage piracy of copyrighted materials, electronically or otherwise. Your support of the author's rights is appreciated.

About AMA
American Management Association (www.amanet.org) is a world leader in talent development, advancing the skills of individuals to drive business success. Our mission is to support the goals of individuals and organizations through a complete range of products and services, including classroom and virtual seminars, webcasts, webinars, podcasts, conferences, corporate and government solutions, business books and research. AMA's approach to improving performance combines experiential learning—learning through doing—with opportunities for ongoing professional growth at every step of one's career journey.

Printing number
10 9 8 7 6 5 4 3 2 1

For Meghan, Molly, and Taylor....

May each of you always follow your unique passions.

UCB
299361

Contents

Acknowledgments

Thanks to:

My parents, Patricia and James, for encouraging me.

Jill Nolan for tons of support, savvy business advice, and tradeshow assistance, and for being such a great sister and aunt to my kids.

Jane Nolan for helping me in so many ways, including giving me her house by the ocean when I needed a quiet place to write, for taking business trips with me, and for being a great sister and aunt to my kids.

My customers, fans, and followers online and in person. I appreciate each and every one of you.

Everyone who told me they wished I would write a book.

All the people I've met along the way who contributed to the wonderful adventures I have been lucky enough to be part of. It has been and continues to be a blast.

Sheree Bykofsky, my accomplished and personable agent, who felt I needed to be published and asked where I had been all her life, because she herself had invented something but didn't know how to proceed. Now she'll know how!

My editor, Ellen Kadin, who acquired this book and is such a nice person as well as a true professional.

Cait Johnson, my collaborator extraordinaire, a match made in heaven.

John McGonagle, my smart and trustworthy patent attorney.

Julia Huston, my brilliant patent and trademark litigator.

Jay Such at Boutwell, Owens & Co., my printers, who treated me like a multimillion-dollar customer even though he knew I was just starting out.

Dawn Kenney at DMK Graphics for getting my artwork into the proper 21st-century files and handling a lot of other crucially important tasks.

LABBB Collaborative Work Training Center staff and students for assembling and packaging some of my products.

And to anyone who was a guinea pig for some of my childhood inventing experiments . . . I hope you are well.

I would also like to express my appreciation to Kevin Dougherty, Susan Huff, John and Kerry at La Muse, and Maria Paone.

Last, and most profoundly, my thanks to Tom, the co-inventor of our three daughters, and to Meghan, Molly, and Taylor, who changed my life in ways I never could have imagined, and whose toys were secretly taken apart for my prototypes on many occasions.

I love you all.

P.S. Thanks to Coconut, too.

Introduction

If the state of the economy is making you lose sleep, take heart: you could probably come up with at least two great ideas right now to turn into a thriving business or the source of abundant royalty checks. So what's stopping you? Maybe you think inventors are either really rich or really special and you're just an ordinary person, so there's no way. Or maybe you're scared you'd have to quit your day job or go into serious hock to get a product off the ground.

Well, there's good news: none of that is true. My message in a nutshell is that anyone can become a successful inventor. Just think "six-plus-six"— six personality traits for success and six simple steps to invention. You don't need a trust fund, a corner office, or a second mortgage to do it. All you need is your own imagination and this book.

Think of *Idea to Invention* as a kind of fertile hybrid of how-to handbook, self-help manual, and motivational inspiration designed to help you to convert your brainwaves into lucrative products—and I've got lots of effective (and cheap!) secrets for creating the independent life you want to live.

Idea to Invention will help you to:

➤ Take charge of your life with empowering tips and easy instructions for creating money with your ideas.

➤ Follow the six simple steps to bring your inventions to fruition.

➤ Harness the power of the Internet to make money and promote your ideas.

➤ Navigate the ins and outs of licensing and patenting your products.

➤ Take the Success Quiz and receive helpful hints to boost your confidence and your success potential.

➤ Stack the deck of luck in your favor.

➤ Ride the waves of inspiration into a more independent and abundant new life.

I've learned the hard way about a lot of stuff you need to know—including the patent process, licensing, manufacturing, social media, and more. And I'm still learning. Surfing the learning curve by myself was challenging, but you won't have to do that; this book makes all of it easy to understand. Because I know some of you are visual learners like me, I made sure to include some eye-catching graphics as well as fun quizzes, fact-filled sidebars, inspirational quotes, often-humorous true stories, helpful exercises, and links to great how-to instructional videos.

I want reading this book to be as much fun as learning how to be an inventor—because it really is an exciting adventure. I designed *Idea to Invention* to inspire and empower you, so you can grab your ideas and run with them all the way to the bank.

If you're wondering why I developed my six simple steps to invention in the first place, the answer is as simple as the steps. It just drives me crazy when I see people who could and should be successful getting overwhelmed and giving up instead. By breaking down the journey to invention into six steps, I've been able to help lots of people make the right moves to convert their ideas into hot, must-have merchandise without getting stuck in the swamps that often lurk on either side of the road to prosperity. I also don't like it when good people get ripped off by con artists.

So why should you listen to me? Because I've sold millions of products, hold multiple patents and trademarks, and for years I've been lighting "You can do it!" motivational fires under groups as different as Fortune 500 CEOs and grade-school kids and have brought my message to radio, television, and the Internet.

Now let's take a look at what you'll find in the coming chapters.

YOU HAVE WHAT IT TAKES TO SUCCEED!

Most people are afraid they lack some mysterious "success gene," but anyone can develop the traits that predict success. I've identified six basic personality traits that appear to be shared by most successful individuals, and I've given them a snappy acronym to make them easy to remember. Take my fun Success Quiz to find out how you rate, then use my great advice for getting those important traits super-buff and toned, so you can get your *Idea to Invention* off the ground and on its way to making profits.

THE SIX SIMPLE STEPS TO INVENTION

I know exactly what it takes to turn ideas into products, and I'll lead you through the process step by fascinating step. You'll master the habits of creative thinkers, seeing everyday problems as opportunities. You'll find out how to get free money to promote your ideas. You'll learn how to make simple mock-up prototypes of your idea so you can start to visualize it displayed at your favorite store. Then you'll find out how to keep your ideas safe from pirates, including how to get a free initial consultation with a patent attorney, and how to register a trademark on your own—all according to your budget and plan for profit. Next you'll learn my secrets for grabbing attention for your product, building buzz with social media, finding store buyers, taking tradeshow shortcuts, and much more. Should you manufacture your product yourself or not? We'll explore the pros and cons of finding a licensed manufacturer or setting up an assembly line in your basement. And finally, you'll add dazzle to your product by thinking like a buyer, dreaming up some bells-and-whistles enhancements that will add shelf life to your product and keep it a hot, must-have item for years to come, giving you multiple streams of income.

I'll show you how to use the (mostly free) power of the Internet to build a platform for your brainchild. And I'll offer my proven helpful hints for living a healthy, happy inventor's life, helping you to embrace the process of being an inventor.

Your own journey will be as unique as your ideas, but the six-plus-six secrets apply to everyone. It's all here. It's all easy. It's all *Idea to Invention*.

CHAPTER 1

My Success Story

If I Can Do It, So Can You

I never dreamed about success. I worked for it.
—ESTEE LAUDER

The first thing you need to know about me is that I'm an ordinary person. I have three kids, I didn't go to Harvard, I don't have a trust fund, and some days I look in the mirror and think I could use a makeover. But I've turned my ideas into products that have sold in the tens of millions and made me a success. I'm living proof that you can create your own American dream. And I figured if I can do that, so can you.

You wouldn't believe how many people want to be inventors! I've been giving inspirational talks about the power of invention to packed houses for years, to everyone from CEOs of big corporations to grade-school kids, and every time I do, people come up to me afterward with questions. Lots of them. Now, I love answering questions, but it hit me that I could put all my answers into a book. That way I could help even more people turn their dreams into products and profits. I like people and I like helping them to attain their goals, so that sounded good to me. And many of the folks I met told me, "You should write a book!" Which explains why you are holding this one in your hands.

Maybe a lot of people want to be inventors simply because inventing is something almost every human can do. We're hardwired to come up with creative solutions to practical problems. But I think inventing also is a hot topic now because we're beginning to see that the big corporations care very little about us as employees. Being your own boss and freeing yourself from dependence on greedy institutions that don't give a damn is starting to sound more and more attractive. The thing is, this world is pretty challenging, and the economy isn't in the greatest shape, so most of us could use some advice on how to make our own way.

That's where this book comes in. I wrote it for everyone. The techniques I share are easy to follow and easy to understand. And they work. How do I know? Because they worked for me, and they've worked for the many people I've spoken to who've tried them.

I'm here to tell you this: You can create the success you want. And you don't have to be rich to do it; you can make a fortune without spending one. I want to motivate you. To inspire you. And to show you step-by-step how it's done.

For me, it all started with a car seat.

Picture this: I'm a new mom. I'm driving in heavy downtown Boston traffic with my precious infant tucked into her gotta-have-one-it's-the-law rear-facing car seat. I don't hear her. Is she breathing? Is she okay? Then she starts whimpering. Is she sick? Has she gotten her head caught in a strap or something? Who can tell? The damned car seat is facing away from me so no matter how much I look in my rearview mirror, I can't see her. One thing you need to know is that I have just a little bit of Irish temper in me. When I finally got my baby and myself safely home, I called my mom to vent. "It's ridiculous!" I fumed. "Somebody should invent some kind of special mirror so you could see your kid in the stupid rear-facing car seat." And, in a moment that has since become family legend, my mom, the prophet from the couch, said, "Uh-hunh. Why don't *you* invent one?"

Wow. And you know what? I did. And the rest, as they say, is history. Millions of sales later, you can look in one of my multi-patented rear-facing car seat mirrors and see little Taylor, or Molly, or Meghan and know that your baby is okay. Or not. And if not, you can pull over and do something about it.

The whole point of this story is that it all started with a need. And that's what gets the ball rolling with most inventions: necessity, the mother of them all. If you need something and it doesn't exist, rather than seeing a problem, see an opportunity. All it takes is one good idea and you can make a difference, fill the need, solve the problem. How exciting and empowering is that?

Of course, brilliant ideas aren't enough. I always think of Edison's famous quote about success being 10 percent inspiration and 90 percent perspiration, and it's true. I got my work ethic from my dad, one of the hardest-working guys I've ever known.

Dad worked full time for a commercial flooring company and then moonlighted after hours doing his own flooring and tile business on the side, but he always had time to play with me and my sisters. Looking back, I'm not sure when the man had time to sleep. But he was the poster child for the notion that loving what you do makes you a better person; he was one of the kindest people I've ever known and we all loved him. And he

was always in my corner. When it came time to start manufacturing my car seat mirrors, he and my mom helped me assemble them.

That leads me to another important point: while you can do it all on your own, it sure helps to have support when you're bringing up a product so it can walk on its own. Besides encouraging me to go to college and make something of myself, my mom helped me with my first graphic design business, answering the phones—and calling herself by another name so nobody would know we were related! She also helped me with my first Boston trade show and was my PR person at local stores, raving about my product to the owners.

I married my childhood sweetheart, and I'm blessed that he's a tremendously supportive husband. He encouraged my ambitions from day one, buying me my very first business suit and a helpful book on self-promotion that I still use today. He escorts me to TV appearances and trade shows, and is generally a fan. Plus my sisters and friends have been hugely helpful.

But remember—even if you don't have the kind of motivational fire in the belly that I learned from my dad, this book will help you fire yourself up, believe in yourself and your ideas, and start changing things one step at a time. And if you don't have family or friends to cheer you on and provide the crucial support I received, you can start by being a one-person cheerleader for yourself.

There's really no excuse for not following your dreams. I started on my own road to success in the days before the Internet, cell phones, or personal computers. Imagine the time and effort you can save with these genies in your corner! Besides, as my mom always says, "Do it now—you could get hit by a bus!"

It all starts with a quiz, so sharpen your pencil. You're about to find out how *you* rate in the success department—and then I'll show you how to make it to the top of the class.

Take the Success Quiz You Can't Fail—

and Learn How to I.N.V.E.N.T.

Let no feeling of discouragement prey upon you, and in the end you are sure to succeed.

—ABRAHAM LINCOLN

If you ask someone the question "Do you have what it takes to succeed?" the answer will probably be a muttered, "I dunno—maybe." Most people don't answer with an emphatic "Yes!" I think that's because of our own beliefs. We really think that successful people are born under some lucky star. Or that they come from wealthy families, with trust funds or probably a rich relative or two waiting in the wings, eager to give them a boost. Or maybe they have some mysterious "success gene"—and, whatever that is, we're pretty sure that the Gene Fairy passed us by when she was giving it out.

Well, think again. Ordinary people create their own success all the time,

just the way I did, and believe me, I didn't have a trust fund, a wealthy uncle, or some success thing encoded in my DNA. I did it all myself, and so can you.

But first, I think we all need to define success for ourselves. So here's a good question to ask yourself: Who are my role models? Because even though we've been taught to think that it's all about millions of dollars and megadoses of power, that isn't always true; there are a lot of rich, powerful people out there who are just plain miserable, and part of success is living a more joyful life.

My favorite role models are women who were told they couldn't make it in a man's world but who did it anyway by following their passion. Julia Child, for instance, created a wonderful life by doing what she loved—cooking French food—and empowering others to do it, too. And I love creative men who think outside the box; for instance, I was absolutely fascinated by the segments on Mister Rogers's television show for children about how things are made. In fact, I have to admit that even now that my children have outgrown him, I still watch him from time to time!

In my years as an inventor and entrepreneur, I've watched a lot of highly successful people complete their marathon run toward success. The journey rarely is a sprint. Real success can take time but, like a slow-growing tree, it creates real, sustainable beauty. And I've learned that the people who achieve joyful, long-lasting success have a lot in common with each other.

In fact, there seem to be six basic personality traits common to most, if not all, successful people, and if you have them, they are your best allies on the road to a vital, joy-filled, and successful life. Figuring this out was really great news—and I was so excited about it that I whipped up a fun quiz so you can see if you have those traits, and find out how strong they are in you.

Even better, this is a quiz you can't fail, since it's just a learning tool to help you see where your success quotient could use a little boost. Most of us could use some help here, which is why the following chapters are designed to support you in getting your success traits really pumped up. Once your success traits are in good shape, you'll be well on your way to becoming the powerhouse you deserve to be and creating the life of creativity and independence you dream of living. With these six personality success traits on your side, anyone can learn how to I.N.V.E.N.T.!

It all starts with the quiz, so grab a pencil.

These are true/false questions. Give yourself one point for every "true" answer. Please try to be as honest as you can. Remember, it doesn't really matter how you score; this book is all about helping you to improve your success quotient!

PART A: INQUISITIVE

TRUE   FALSE

❏   ❏   I like to try new things; I dislike feeling that I'm in a rut.

❏   ❏   I approach life with curiosity—I can't wait to see what will happen next.

❏   ❏   I usually view problems as opportunities for coming up with solutions, or for learning something new.

❏   ❏   I'm mostly up for a challenge because I love to figure things out.

❏   ❏   I often notice ordinary household products that could use some improvement and wonder how I'd go about it.

❏   ❏   If I don't know the answer to something, I like to go online to find out—or look it up in a book, or ask a friend or an expert. I enjoy learning stuff.

PART B: NERVE

TRUE FALSE

❏ ❏ When I meet with criticism, I remind myself that I can learn something from it.

❏ ❏ I don't take rejection personally.

❏ ❏ I tend to have a fairly sturdy self-image: in general, I like myself.

❏ ❏ People tell me I'm pretty self-confident.

❏ ❏ I know I have something to offer.

❏ ❏ I'm not afraid to present my ideas to total strangers. After all, nothing ventured, nothing gained!

PART C: VOICE

TRUE FALSE

❏ ❏ I'm not shy about speaking up in public.

❏ ❏ I think most people find me interesting and likable.

❏ ❏ When I talk, people really pay attention to me.

❏ ❏ I enjoy opportunities to share my thoughts and ideas.

❏ ❏ I don't need to be loud or pushy to be an effective communicator—people relate to me.

❏ ❏ I love to share my enthusiasm and passion with others.

PART D: ENERGY

TRUE   FALSE

❏   ❏   I tend to be a highly motivated person.

❏   ❏   If I get tired or downhearted, I know what to do to pick
              myself back up and recharge.

❏   ❏   I'm good at pacing myself.

❏   ❏   I am generally positive and optimistic.

❏   ❏   I usually have enough energy to do what I want to do.

❏   ❏   When I'm doing something I love, I feel absolutely filled with
              vitality.

PART E: NOURISH

TRUE   FALSE

❏   ❏   I love to be inspired and I know what lights me up.

❏   ❏   I'm good at imagining what I want to happen.

❏   ❏   I feel encouraged by others' success stories.

❏   ❏   I foster relationships that support my dreams, rather than
              spending time with people who rain on my parade.

❏   ❏   I know where to go and what to do to feel empowered.

❏   ❏   I get a lot of satisfaction whenever I accomplish something.

PART F: TENACITY

TRUE   FALSE

❏   ❏   Every time I hit a roadblock in my plans, I see it as an opportunity to rethink and go a different way.

❏   ❏   I think most people give up too easily. I don't.

❏   ❏   I don't mind revising outdated dreams. I'm smart enough to go on to a new idea rather than hitting my head against a brick wall or losing everything.

❏   ❏   Delays in reaching my goals are just a sign that I need to try harder.

❏   ❏   I love creative problem solving—it's fun for me.

❏   ❏   I don't have any specific time frame for achieving my objectives. It will take as long as it takes.

ANSWERS

Add 'em up and see how many points you have for each part.

Part A: Inquisitive

Endless curiosity is one of the most important characteristics of an inventive and successful person.

0 – Okay, don't worry, Chapter 3 will help.

1 – There is always hope!

2 – It's a start!

3 – Not bad!

4 – Good!

5 – Great!

6 – Fabulous!

Part B: Nerve

Having a sturdy self-image, and learning not to take rejection personally, is vital to success.

0 – Don't panic; just read Chapter 4.

1 – There is always hope!

2 – It's a start!

3 – Not bad!

4 – Good!

5 – Great!

6 – Fabulous!

Part C: Voice

Knowing how to make yourself heard—and that doesn't mean yelling!—is crucial if you want to be successful.

0 – You can learn how to be listened to. Chapter 5 will help you to develop a stronger voice.

1 – There is always hope!

2 – It's a start!

3 – Not bad!

4 – Good!

5 – Great!

6 – Fabulous!

Part D: Energy

Successful people know how to energize themselves—in fact, they get a lot of their vitality from doing what they love.

0 – No problem; Chapter 6 will help to fire you up.
1 – There is always hope!
2 – It's a start!
3 – Not bad!
4 – Good!
5 – Great!
6 – Fabulous!

Part E: Nourish

Knowing how to support your creative thinking by feeding your self, your life, and your imagination is a vital key to success.

0 – Chapter 7 will show you how to feed your dreams.
1 – There is always hope!
2 – It's a start!
3 – Not bad!
4 – Good!
5 – Great!
6 – Fabulous!

Part F: Tenacity

When the going gets tough, the successful know how to keep at it.

0 – Don't give up! Chapter 8 will help you find some real stick-to-it determination.

1 – There is always hope!

2 – It's a start!

3 – Not bad!

4 – Good!

5 – Great!

6 – Fabulous!

Now that you know how you rate, you can read the chapters that follow to improve your score, and get ready for the six simple steps to invention.

Are You **I**nquisitive? Cultivate Curiosity!

I think, at a child's birth, if a mother could ask a fairy godmother to endow it with the most useful gift, that gift would be curiosity.

—ELEANOR ROOSEVELT

An inventor's best friend is curiosity. In fact, that may be the single most important trait for any human being. Why? Because it's the spark that adds meaning and interest to life. Remember when you were a kid and you wanted to know everything? Why is the sky blue? What makes grass green? Why does it get dark at night? Children are just naturally inquisitive and they're interested in everything. Very young children are never bored—they're too busy discovering things. Sadly, most of us seem to lose this sense of wonder as we grow older.

That's too bad, because being inquisitive gets the creative juices flowing, and it can feed our product ideas in unexpected and fascinating ways. Think of Steve Jobs. He took a class in calligraphy at Reed College for no other reason than he liked the way calligraphy looked and he was curious about it. I'm sure there were plenty of people in his life who told him, "Man, you're wasting your time there, Steve." But ten years later, he designed the first Mac's typography around what he had learned.

If you wonder how things work, and you follow your curiosity, you never know where the information you gather will lead you. When my daughter Molly was little, one of her favorite things was an origami paper-folding kit and book. I was curious about it and found myself inexplicably drawn to fiddling with it—and years later, when I wanted to design a dog waste bag with a cardboard collar, I realized origami held the answer to the burning question, "How do I fold this so it's nice and compact?" More recently, I picked up a brochure about free conversational French being offered at my local library and decided to take the classes. And then I ended up unexpectedly going to France, where I went on a writer/artist retreat and germinated the idea of this book. Not only that, I just took a blacksmithing course for no other reason than I was inquisitive about it. Now I'm wondering how I'll use what I learned later on!

So how do we grow a fine crop of curiosity? Here's how to start.

THE CURIOSITY JOURNAL

Many inventive types have a blank book (or two or thirty) that we use to jot down anything that intrigues us. We make a habit not only of keeping them, but of rereading them every so often. And it's amazing how many times I find myself saying, "Oh my gosh! I'd forgotten all about that. But what a great question/idea/concept. In fact, that might help me with the widget I'm in the midst of designing!"

THE LIFETIME LEARNING LIST

Inventors know one thing for sure: we don't know it all! In fact, there is a fascinating world of stuff to find out about that's just waiting for us to get our curiosity in gear. So, without overthinking too much, make a list *right now* of at least three things you'd like to learn more about, just because you're curious about them (my list would include how to weld and shape metal for metal sculptures, the Tiny Home movement, and beautiful places to travel to and live in for a while). Write them in your Curiosity Journal. And find out more about them if you can.

ASK QUESTIONS

When you meet new people, ask questions about what they do and how they do it. If they're not part of the workforce, ask about their hobbies and passions. You'll find that most people love to talk about what interests and excites them. An added advantage, especially if you're a little shy or introverted, is that this simple technique will make the folks you meet think you're brilliant without your having to talk too much yourself. No matter what they do or who they are, one thing people share is a deep desire to be heard and seen, so anyone who really listens to other people will automatically score big points. And you'll learn things you may never have even thought of!

Also, asking questions can be just plain useful. Back when I was working as a graphic artist for a small company, we were always calling someone to come fix the typesetting machine. I watched the guy while he worked and politely asked questions. Years later, when I started my own business, I bought a reconditioned machine from that same guy and I was actually able to fix it myself!

READ AND RESEARCH

Go to a bookstore or library and browse. Pick up magazines or books that intrigue you and use your Curiosity Journal to jot down anything that piques your interest. Read everything you can lay your hands on—and research like a maniac! This is key: if you read enough you don't need to hire an "expert" at every step; you'll be your own expert. Back in the day, I hung out every chance I got at the Boston Public Library, usually with a baby in a backpack and a toddler in a stroller. When the treats I'd brought for them ran out and the fussing started, I had to go home. Now I can look up just about anything at my own desk. I love the Internet! What a gift!

JUMP-START YOUR CONSUMER CURIOSITY

Make it a habit to examine the labels on every product you routinely buy. Start asking, "Why?" and "What does *this* do?" or "Why doesn't it include____?" You'll start to see that a lot of products contain exactly the same ingredients; it's packaging and marketing that often make things sell.

Once you've whetted your curiosity about the things you usually purchase, extend it to products you don't routinely buy. Visit specialty stores. What's selling? What's missing from the shelves? What do you wish you saw? What do you think might be needed? What makes a product stand out? What makes you want to buy it? What trends do you notice? Check out colors and styles. What's in fashion? Right now, "earth-friendly" is a biggie. And so are "natural ingredients." Chapter 16, on how to build the right platform for you, will show you how to check out hashtags to find out what's hot and trending.

If you have a product idea in mind, check out the stores where you'd like to see it on the shelves. When I was developing my baby car seat mirror, I used to haunt the baby section—and the automotive section!—of all the local department stores, checking out packaging, size, price, and possible competition. I learned a lot about what looked good, what had customer appeal, and what didn't.

You don't always have to reinvent the wheel, either: sometimes you can profit from taking an existing product and improving it. After all, a market already exists for it, so that's a plus. And people love "new and improved" anything! But first you have to ask, "What does this product need in order for it to be better?" A friend recently noticed that I'm constantly picking up products in any store I'm in, and studying them to see how they function, how they're made, and what they do. It's become second nature. You can do it, too.

TRUST YOUR OWN INTERESTS

Rumi, the great mystic poet, said, "Let yourself be silently drawn by the stronger pull of what you really love." Which means go for what attracts you, follow your heart and your interests, trust that what intrigues you has

something to teach or show you, even if others think you're nuts. Think of Bethenny Frankel, the reality TV star and talk-show host. She was curious about what it would be like to tend bar, so she took a bartending course—and years later she invented and sold her *Skinny Girl Margarita* to a top player in the alcohol industry, proving all the people wrong who had told her, "This business is dominated by men. You don't have a chance." She trusted herself and let herself be guided by what interested her—just as Steve Jobs did with the calligraphy.

Even if you can't imagine what possible use it may have, give yourself the gift of following up on the stuff that you're curious about, as often as you possibly can.

TRUST SYNCHRONICITY

Synchronicity is a funny thing. Sometimes you'll have no idea why something suddenly appears on your radar screen, only to discover a few months later that it holds the key to a splendid new idea. And I've noticed that the more you trust yourself and the things that just "accidentally" cross your path, the more wonderful synchronous stuff starts to happen: books fall open at just the right page, products practically leap off the shelves, a friend "just happens" to mention something that solves a problem. Like magic.

Not only that, trusting synchronicity can lead to some very happy "accidents"—because did you know that many popular products were invented by accident? Take Post-it Notes, for instance. The 3M company was really looking for a super-strong adhesive, not something you could peel right off. And Silly Putty was a by-product of an attempt to manufacture synthetic rubber for the war effort in the 1940s. So it pays to be curious and open to the unexpected.

Also, synchronicity can sometimes lead to improvements you never even imagined. When I was assembling my car seat mirror, I was curious to see if I could eliminate the use of adhesive, so I researched a bunch of different ways to attach two pieces of plastic inexpensively. The "Aha!" was that I could put holes in both pieces and attach them using rivets and a cheap rivet gun. It worked! But the extra bonus was that the rivet allowed the mirror to be adjustable—an advantage I had never foreseen.

Now that your Curiosity Garden is blooming nicely, and you're jotting things down in your Curiosity Journal like a fiend, asking questions, reading and researching, and checking out every product that comes your way, it's time to goose up your nerve. Read on!

4

Do You Have **N**erve?
Grow a Thicker Skin!

You will never do anything in this world without courage. It is the greatest quality of the mind next to honor.

—ARISTOTLE

It really bugs me when I think of all the people I've met who have wonderful, cool, or valuable ideas but lack the self-confidence to put them out there. The world loses out on so much that could be useful or beautiful or helpful. To paraphrase the great modern dancer, Martha Graham, the imaginative life force flows through you and because there is only one of you, your expression of that force is absolutely unique—so if you block your own self-expression, it will never exist in the form that only you could give it. The world will lose out on it. Stop worrying about whether it's "good" or not, or if it's as good as somebody else's expression. Getting caught in fretting about whether or not you measure up to somebody else is such a trap. As writer and artist William Blake said almost two hundred years ago, "I will not reason or compare: my business is to create." I think I should have that tattooed on my forehead.

A friend of mine told me about a great dream she had. It was one of those where you're on stage (analogous to the one where you're standing in front of an examination committee) and you don't know what you're doing. You don't know the answers. You don't know your lines. So there she was in the spotlight in this dream with the audience all sitting there in front of her waiting for her to perform and she didn't have a foggy clue what she was supposed to do. And suddenly she thought, "Wait a minute. I'm dreaming. I can do whatever I want!" And she spread her arms, opened her mouth, and belted out her favorite song. Because what the heck? It was just a dream and she could do whatever she liked.

If we all approached life like this—with a "What the heck" attitude— more great inventions and more creative works would get shared. If we could only divorce our vulnerable egos from our ideas, we would be unstoppable. And that's what this chapter will help you do. We're all sensitive. We all hate rejection. But there's a way around it.

DETACH

Most of us *identify* with our ideas, the darling children of our imaginations. A rude or indifferent response to an idea of ours can send us straight back to childhood, when we were taunted or misunderstood, when words not only hurt us but left us scarred for life. Ugh, who needs that? So, many of us just clam up and refuse to give the world a chance to inflict any more pain.

But what if you let go and allowed creative ideas to simply flow through you? Then your creative offspring aren't really "yours." You do your best by them, of course, but if they get rejected, it doesn't mean you're worthless. It just means you need to shrug, learn what you can from the rejection, tightly hold on to your belief in yourself, and keep on trying to be a nurturing conduit for your free-flowing ideas.

You need to do this because all of us have some responsibility to the world—to making it a better, safer, kinder, more beautiful place. In a way, concentrating on our fragile little feelings is a disservice to why we were put here—to enjoy life, to do what we love best, and to make a positive difference if we can.

It's a practice that gets easier with time. The less we attach to specific outcomes even as we continue putting our ideas out there, the easier it gets. The secret is to keep taking forward-moving steps no matter what. Sometimes that means dropping an idea and turning your attention to another. In Chapter 11, I'll help you figure out whether you should keep going with a particular idea or let it go and move on to your next one.

STOP OFFERING YOUR JUGULAR TO THE VAMPIRES—AND KNOW YOUR CHEERLEADERS!

Before we can work on developing what it takes to approach a potential buyer or manufacturer, there may be some work that needs to be done closer to home.

First of all, it's not advisable to tell anybody your specific product ideas (this is called "public disclosure") because it could ruin your chances for getting a patent. It's important to protect your ideas—but I'll tell you more about that in Chapter 12. That said, it's okay to speak generally to your loved ones, and to tell them that you have a dream—a dream to invent a product and sell it and see it on shelves everywhere.

The trouble is, many of you have friends or relatives who might habitually dump on those dreams. Most of us have people in our lives who poison our confidence with comments like, "I don't think you have it in you to do that—remember, you almost flunked algebra in 8th grade," or "I'm sure somebody's already thought of anything you'd invent," or, even worse, "Who do you think you are?" We need all of this about as much as we need the proverbial crater in the cranium. I always think of the example of Mrs. Fields, the cookie maven, who was told that her business would never take off because the idea was stupid, she didn't have a college degree, and she had no money. So much for those people.

After I had a patent pending and had started manufacturing my car seat mirror, a family member with a snazzy new car told me that her husband would never attach my product to their car upholstery. I think because they didn't have an infant, they didn't realize how necessary my product was, and now, millions of sales later, I can smile and think, "Wow, was she ever wrong!" I'm so glad I didn't let her stop me.

A good first step in developing nerve is to identify the people in our lives who don't understand us or our idea, or who don't really want us to succeed for whatever reason—and then stop giving away our energy to them.

You may still be married or related to one of those people, or have the occasional cup of coffee with some of them, but they do not deserve to hear your creative hopes. Stop exposing yourself *right now* to anyone who doesn't give the correct response. The best-case correct response is, "I'm sure you can do it!" At worst, it might be "I'm intrigued. Can you tell me more about what you hope to do?" Anyone who responds like this is a cheerleader, and we need a real connection with those, so that when we meet with the occasional bump in the road, we can reach out to them—and they can help us turn ughs into hugs. The litmus test here is, are these people genuinely interested in and curious about us and our aims? We're not expecting them to rave about every single brainwave, but at least they should want to know more about what we have in mind.

The truth is, many people will feel threatened by your courage in pursuing anything new. They worry that you're bigger than they are and they want to keep you as small and dull as they feel. So the next time someone close to you derides an ambition of yours, just look at them with compassion and remind yourself that they must feel really insecure to do that to your exciting, innovative, creative self. And remember that their opinion has nothing whatsoever to do with your journey.

Several years ago, a "good friend" walked into my office (which was loaded with my products). When during our conversation I told her I was thinking about writing a book, she actually told me I had delusions of grandeur. To tell you the truth, it stopped me in my tracks for a few. But eventually I realized her comment shouldn't have had the power to affect me the way it did, so I picked myself up and kept going. If I had listened to her, you wouldn't be reading this book right now. (As my mom would say, "She's just jealous!")

REFRAME CRITICISM

There's a big difference between the knee-jerk "I don't think so!" nonsense that our nearest and dearest sometimes dish out and the thoughtful criticism of People in Power (and you won't be reaching out to them until you have a patent pending or you have them sign a non-disclosure agreement—but you'll find out more about this in Chapter 12). Although it's never fun to hear that your concept isn't perfect exactly the way it is, if we think of criticism from those in the know as helpful suggestions instead of barbed arrows of negativity, those people just may help us to improve our product.

So before you throw everything someone says out the window, jot it down. Give yourself a day or two to recover, and then look at what was said objectively. If this weren't *your* brainchild—if you were a completely detached observer—would anything your critic said make sense? Could that person have a point? How could that be used to improve your idea?

Here's an example: Back in the day, I got in touch with a bigwig buyer for a chain of famous baby-products stores. I asked this man if I could come present my car seat mirror product to him and he said, "Sure. It's your dime." So, five months pregnant, I flew to New Jersey, spent even more money and time in a cab, and arrived in this man's office only to find him chugging directly from a bottle of bright pink antacid. Clearly this was a bad day for him, and I was exhausted, but I made my pitch anyway. Although his response was less than enthusiastic—for one thing, he suggested I change the packaging—he did admit the product had merit, and that was really encouraging. I got the feeling the chain wanted a manufacturer with a line of products and huge manufacturing capabilities, but I refused to give up. When I got home, I zoomed over to one of the stores and studied which companies might like my mirror as an extension of their line. I found the contact info on the back of each product, and cold-called each company. In the meantime I was told by one of my customers that I should be at an international trade show for baby products in Dallas. I found out how to get a booth and I went. Long story short, I don't know if it was the trade show or the cold-call pitch, but I attracted the attention of a licensee, who changed the packaging and cleverly framed the mirror so it looked like it was being held by an adorable stuffed animal. They were open to working with me and valued my input on every level—we both were excited to find each other. My product ended up in the very chain of stores (and many more) whose buyer had originally rejected it—but with different packaging and a bunch of bells-and-whistles variations (like a light-up version for night driving)! For more about improving and enhancing your product to keep it selling, see Chapter 15.

FIND THE RIGHT APPROACH

This section has two important parts. First, instead of thinking of yourself as going hat-in-hand with a big, needy *"Please take my product"* sign around your neck, think of it this way: your product could make a lot of money for these people! In fact, it could be the best thing since Otto Rohwedder's bread-slicing machine. Will they do the right thing by your idea? Are they good enough to represent it or carry it? If they don't take it, it's just a sign that there's somebody better out there, somebody who will be a better match.

The second important aspect of this right-approach thing is to *do your research* so you can present your idea in a way that will appeal or make sense to the person you're showing it to. And if you get a rejection, don't be deterred: go to the next organization on your list, where it might be a perfect fit. I'll tell you more about how to present your product in the most effective way in Chapter 13.

CELEBRATE YOUR CREATIONS

Here's a concept I really love: Create a little "shrine" somewhere in your home or office with objects on it that remind you of your accomplishments

so that every time you see it, you can say, "Wow! I did this!" If you don't like the idea of a shrine, then keep a Success Journal and record in it all of the things you've created or done—and this can include things like, "I made that phone call even though I was nervous!" or "I figured out a way to package this so it's less expensive."

The most important thing to remember about strengthening your nerve is that the combination of detachment from your ideas, the desire to learn from feedback—both positive and negative—and an unshakable *intention* to invent will see you through. Sometimes we just need to shrug and say, "Oh well!" and imagine a different concept. The source of creative ideas is limitless.

When you're ready to share your product with the world, you'll need a voice that others will listen to. Next I'll show you how to speak up!

CHAPTER
5

How Strong Is Your **V**oice? Passion Speaks!

Stand upright, speak thy thoughts, declare the truth thou hast, that all may share; Be bold, proclaim it everywhere: They only live who dare.

—VOLTAIRE

A few decades ago, several books came out popularizing a concept that was revolutionary at the time: we learned that we could read other people's body language to find out what they're really saying because, although words may lie, the body never does. Along with that novel idea goes this one: We can recognize the ring of truth in words spoken with passionate conviction. And that's what "voice" in this chapter is all about—not learning how to sugarcoat or "spin" the truth, or how to lie to get what we want, but how to connect with our truth and our energy.

Energy is contagious: when we are enthusiastic ourselves, we can convince others. When we deeply believe in our idea, even if we have moments of insecurity or low self-confidence, we can convince others. No matter how shy or quiet you are, you can develop a strong voice—remember, strong doesn't automatically mean loud—that will give you a better chance of getting others to really *hear* what you have to say. It's a three-step proposition: We have to know ourselves and understand what motivates us to speak out. We have to condense what we say down to its simplest, strongest bones. And we have to feel passionate about what we say.

Follow these three steps and you'll be unstoppable. Even if you don't always get the reaction from your listener that you want (and many factors can affect others' reactions, most of them having absolutely nothing to do with you), your inner self will hear what you say and it will start waving pom-poms and cheering you on. This builds confidence. You will begin to see yourself as someone who speaks the truth with conviction, who advocates for your ideas with energy and dynamism. Soon your self-esteem will soar.

1. WHAT MAKES *YOU* TALK?

There are scores of online tests you can take to find out your personality type, but it's also useful to find out what motivates you to talk to others. Here's a simple little quiz to get you thinking, so you can do what Dolly Parton suggests: find out who you are and do it on purpose. Before you even open your mouth, it's good to know what you really want. Then you can learn to communicate—and fulfill your goals—in a more focused and effective way.

Your (Very Short and Simple) Communication Motivation Quiz

The title is almost as long as the quiz! But this will help you to discover what motivates you to communicate.

True or False?

➤ I love showing people how to do things, teaching them and giving out useful information. (Teacher)

➤ I love lighting people up and empowering them with ideas and possibilities. (Inspirer)

➤ I love to be of service, helping people to improve their lives. (Helper)

➤ I love to connect emotionally with people and create networks of connection between others. (Connector)

If you answered "True" to all the statements, that would be ideal, since even though these one-word "types" may be pretty obvious, a strong voice should include elements of all of them. But even if you only had one "true," pat yourself on the back right now for having at least one strong motivation that will help get you energized about your product or idea. If you know for a fact that you're a Helper type, for instance, you'll find it easy to tailor what you say to show others how your idea will make things better for them. If you're a Teacher, you'll shine at sharing the facts and information that will interest and fascinate others. If you're a Connector, you can easily get people to like and trust you. And if you're an Inspirer, you'll get them fired up about your project. Most of us come into the game already strong in one or two of these areas, and that's good because these characteristics will come in handy when you present your product to anyone who will listen! (See Chapter 13.)

2. FIND THE BONES

Every day we are bombarded with talk. Between the Internet, TV's talking heads, and radio newscasters and DJs, the stream of words is endless—and we are burning out with information overload. So what do we do? We tune it out. Life is too short to listen to every little word, especially when those words mean nothing to us. Do you remember the "Peanuts" cartoons, where the teacher's voice sounded like "wah, waaah, wah"? That's our world. So what do you do if you have something to say and you want people to listen? First, you cut away all the blah-blah.

So here's a useful little concept that will help you whittle things down to essentials. It's called an "elevator pitch." The premise is that you're in an elevator and an important and possibly helpful-to-you person gets on and, wonder of wonders, asks you what you're working on. You have maybe 30 seconds before the elevator doors open and out the person goes. So whatever you say has to be as fascinating, punchy, and concise as it can possibly be.

When I first got started I certainly didn't have an elevator pitch, and most of you probably don't either. In fact, if somebody had asked me about my product, my reply would probably have sounded something like this: "So, yah, you know how babies have to be in rear-facing car seats when you take them out in the car, right? And when they're in those car seats, you can't see them. So I'm a mom and I was driving in heavy traffic once and my baby was being really quiet and she usually isn't. So, um, I got worried and there was no way I could see her and I thought, this is nuts, somebody ought to invent a mirror so you could see your baby. My mother asked me why didn't I invent one. So I did. You stick it right on the car upholstery and it works great."

A publicist I met at a gathering once said there are three questions you have to answer in order to promote your product: So what? Who cares? What's in it for me? A good elevator pitch answers those questions with very few words. And that holds true whether you're pitching a novel or your latest widget.

Fast-forward several years. Now my pitch would sound more like this: "By law, babies have to be placed in rear-facing car seats, but parents worry when they can't see their children. I've developed a special mirror so they can. As a mom myself I can tell you it's a huge help."

What a difference from the first example! It has fewer than half the number of words and a lot more energy and punch. It answers the questions by starting off with a fact that tells us "So what" (rear-facing car seats are the law), then connects the listener to emotion/caring (parental worry when you can't see your child), and finally offers a solution that works (what's in it for me). All in about 40 words.

Here's a helpful exercise to try:

Write an elevator pitch of your own about your idea or product. Now detach and look at it with a fresh eye, as if somebody else had written it. Does it answer the three questions? Make sure it does. Now cut it in half. It can be a fun puzzle to see how few words you can use to promote your product!

In Chapter 13, I'll give you lots of tips for using your new sleek-and-streamlined pitch to its best advantage.

3. IGNITE THE PASSION—BUT DITCH YOUR EGO AT THE DOOR

Nothing excites people like excitement and enthusiasm. Those qualities are literally contagious, and in a good way! If you're really fired up by your idea—and not puffed up by your own self-importance—that energy will transmit itself to your listeners. But it is crucial to detach your ego from your idea so you can present that idea as something wonderful and separate from you.

There is one true or false statement that I didn't include in the Communication Motivation Quiz, and that is "I love the idea of being rich, powerful, and superior to others." There's a lot of that out there, and it's the least likely motivator when it comes to feeding your soul and getting you what you want (hence all the rich people who are miserable despite their wealth). Hey, having more than enough is a great idea, but we can't make our lives just about money. Humans are evolved to be part of a community, and to feel that we're making a positive difference.

The truth is, nobody likes an "it's all about *me*" self-promoter. Here's an example of what I mean. When I was on a writer/artist retreat a few years ago, we all had to introduce ourselves and give a quick description of what we were working on. Everyone was great and interesting—except one guy, who went on and on about himself and had an elitist "I am so great" attitude from the get-go. I could see from everyone's faces that we were all turned off. He was so pompous, nobody wanted to listen to him. It could be argued that people who behave this way are really insecure and trying to cover it up, and this is usually true. If only he had decided before he opened his mouth that it was the *work* that was important, not his own fragile little ego! The fine line between self-confidence and humility is one we all need to tread. What really got everyone's juices flowing at the writer/

artist retreat was the obvious passion each creative person had for her or his work. They were so lit up when they talked that I wanted to know more, and I wanted to see—and buy!— their creations for myself, and I found myself warming to each one of them. That's what we're aiming for here. The truth is, while buyers, potential licensees, or manufacturers will want to know how your idea will make money for them, it is just as important that they like you. Sure, they want people who know their stuff, but it's crucial that they see you as someone they could partner with. Your idea may be fantastic, but if you're a royal pain, you're out of the game. The TV show *Shark Tank* proves my point: an inventor who gets too greedy loses out because unbridled ego gets in the way.

PLAY TO YOUR TYPE

Think carefully about the results of your Communication Motivation Quiz. If you're a Helper type but you don't really know what good your product will do—or, worse, if you're secretly afraid it may be bad for people—your ambivalence will show when you talk about it. If you're an Inspirer but are bored by your idea, how on earth will you get anybody else excited about it? I know how important it is to me to galvanize and motivate people. After a radio show or a lecture, I always hear comments like, "Your enthusiasm is so contagious! I want to invent things myself!" That's worth gold to me. And the fact that I get paid makes it even better.

The more we know about ourselves and our deeper motivation, the more authentic—and contagious!—our passion will be. Like body language, the energy of inner strength and conviction can't be faked, and the vibrant, alive energy that comes from being authentic is exactly what the world hungers for. When we create ideas and products from that energy, the world benefits.

Here's a helpful little exercise to strengthen your voice:

See if you can remember a piece of good news about someone else that you were excited about and proud to share. Maybe it was your daughter bringing home a good report card, or your friend or spouse getting a promotion. Now remember the energy in your voice when you told others about it. I'll bet your eyes sparkled and your face was animated and alive. Feel it in your body: try to imitate it with your facial expression and body language. Now imagine feeling this very same energy and aliveness when you talk about a product or idea you've invented.

Find a trusted friend or loved one (a cheerleader!) and try delivering your elevator pitch to that person with that same level of excitement—or practice in front of a mirror. You could even take a video of yourself and see how you come across.

In the next chapter, I'll show you how to tap into your inner Source so you can be an effortless channel for enthusiasm and energy.

6

How's Your **E**nergy Level? Fire It Up!

Energy and persistence conquer all things.

—BEN FRANKLIN

Okay, now you know that accessing your energy is the key if you want to have a voice that people will listen to. So how do you do that? I've boiled it all down to a list of fun things for you to try. Energy needs a healthy body as the vehicle, so some of these tips are simply body-based and health-promoting. Others are about changing your frame of mind. Still others are more about generally fanning the flame that some people call "spirit." Although I think that body, mind, and spirit are all interconnected, I've found it helpful to break things down into categories so we don't feel overwhelmed.

For the most part, all of these ideas are simple and easy to do, but they take practice and a commitment to doing them until they become good habits. I've tried them all, and most are now part of my daily routine, so I don't even have to think about it anymore—I just reap the benefits. How do I know they work? Because my boundless energy is one of the things people notice first about me, and I want you to have it, too!

THE ENERGIZING TO-DO LIST

Body

■ *Breathe deeply.* Make it a practice to take deep breaths as often as you think about it. It's simple physiology: getting more oxygen to your cells is energizing. Whenever I have to sit at my desk for any length of time, I pause every few minutes to take a couple of good deep breaths. A friend of mine lives near a church that has bells tolling the half hour and hour. She says every time she hears the bells, it reminds her to breathe deeply.

■ *Take a walk.* A 30-minute walk every day can keep your mind alert and your blood pumping beautifully, and your walk time is perfect for solving problems and coming up with creative ideas.

■ *Take a nap.* NASA recently discovered that 26-minute naps increased alertness by 54 percent, and performance by 34 percent. Power naps have been the secret of many a genius, including Leonardo da Vinci, Salvador Dali, and Thomas Edison. Some research suggests that 10-minute naps work just as well.

■ *Take a bath.* Albert Einstein did a lot of great thinking in the tub (maybe after his power nap!), and he wasn't the only famous person who did. The famous mystery novelist Agatha Christie, for example, wrote most of her books in the bath.

■ *Drink coffee and eat dark chocolate.* Good coffee and low-sugar dark chocolate go a long way toward energizing many of us (as the great composer J.S. Bach famously said, "Bring me a bowl of coffee before I turn into a goat.") And, sure, we can laugh at those "coffee achiever" ads, but it turns out there's something to them. Over-caffeinating can be bad for your health, though, so use moderation and good sense.

■ *Take a dance break: Put on your headphones and a super-rhythmic song and move it!* Dancing to old-time rock and roll that has a definite beat is an instant energizer for me.

■ *Chew gum!* Some researchers have found that test scores improve when students chew gum; it's now thought that gum-chewing actually boosts our brain power because it increases blood flow to the brain.

■ *Use it or lose it: Do something really sweat-making every once in a while.* I took kickboxing after I had one of my kids to get back in shape, and it really fired me up! Now I go to the gym.

■ *Take a short drive.* Sometimes just having a different view to look at can clear your mind.

■ *Care for a companion animal.* Whenever I see how excited my dog gets when she does the same things over and over, I'm reminded that I don't need to be bored by repetition, and walking her is a great energizer and a good excuse to get a little fresh air twice a day. But whether you favor dogs, cats, or iguanas, there's nothing like giving and receiving unconditional love to create more good energy.

■ *Drink energizing herbal teas.* Make a cup of energizing herbal tea using any combination of the following herbs (or use them in your cooking): dill, bay, chives, cilantro, cinnamon, garlic, ginger, leek, onion, oregano, parsley, peppermint, rosemary, sage.

■ *Use citrus essential oils.* The fragrance of all-natural citrus oils is energizing, so sprinkle a few drops of lemon, lime, orange, or grapefruit oil in a saucer and place it by your desk.

■ *Eat colorfully.* It will help if you eat plenty of leafy greens and colorful vegetables and fruits. The basic rule is to avoid anything white—white flour products like pasta or bread, white sugar, and dairy products loaded with antibiotics and hormones. Avoid sugar, especially. Yes, it gives us an energy rush but it's temporary and usually followed by a crash.

A few years ago, I traveled to a small village in southwestern France. I was there for three weeks, and while I was there, I ate eggs gathered from local chickens, fresh-baked bread, local cheese, and fruit picked right off the trees. Everyone I met was slender and fit, as a result of walking up steep streets and tending gardens, and eating all-natural unprocessed food. Many villagers were in their late eighties and they were still active and full of energy. What an eye-opener! I'm now a big proponent of going back to a healthier diet and lifestyle. One woman I met told me how proud she was that the residents of the village had refused to allow a fast-food chain to come into the area. Even a hipster rock musician kid in his twenties had the same opinion.

Mind

■ Remember that a lot of what we're talking about here is in your head. Energy is a state of mind: staying optimistic and hopeful, focusing on good outcomes, spending time doing things you love, and avoiding the stuff that depletes you will go a long way toward energizing you and keeping you that way.

■ Cultivate a sense of humor. We all face challenges—but they don't have to sap our energy. Believe me, I have been thrown some difficult stuff, but I don't let it extinguish my goals and dreams. In fact I think any struggle can actually give you more drive and purpose, especially if we can laugh about it.

■ Spend time *every day* thinking about or doing things that light you up. Trust your instincts on this: what do you love to do? I love learning new things, so in my free time, I usually do online research or go to my local bookstore or library and browse. I always emerge feeling inspired and lively—when a new idea or concept comes into my head, I feel more spacious, somehow.

■ Most of us imagine the worst-case scenarios constantly, and that's a huge energy drain. Instead, spend time imagining positive outcomes! This will flood your body with feel-good neurochemicals.

■ When you catch yourself thinking a negative thought, switch the channel by doing something positive: call a friend, do a little vacuuming, or read an inspiring book.

Spirit

■ Subscribe to the two-column approach to life. In Column A there are the things we really need to do, like eating, doing laundry, paying bills. Then there's Column B: all the things we love doing and really *want* to do. Sadly, most of us waste our energy somewhere in the middle, doing things we think we "should" do, things that we don't really want to do, and don't really have to do. Stop. Keep your activities in Column A and Column B only—and make an effort to do more Column B stuff.

■ Go on a news fast. All that relentlessly bad news can really drain your spirit after a while.

■ Change something: your routine, your furniture placement, heck, even a drawer in your chest of drawers. This will form new neural pathways and loosen up old, rigid, stuck ways of being, making it easier for creative ideas to come in.

■ Stay busy. The old adage, "If you want to get something done, ask a busy person" is true—the busier you are, the more energy you generate.

■ Avoid people who kvetch incessantly. I read some online research recently suggesting that being around constantly negative people actually shrinks areas of your brain. Even if that's bogus, I can tell you from personal experience that when I weed out interactions with complainers, I feel better.

■ Seek reminders that you and your ego are not the biggest things in the universe. Look at the stars at night. Seek out places of beauty, either in nature, or made by people, and hang out there.

■ Practice an attitude of gratitude. Next time you're driving somewhere, play the Gratitude Game and try listing out loud as many things you're thankful for as you can—and see how many miles you can go before you run dry. This can be large or small stuff, anything from your family or your health to the wildflowers by the side of the road to the color of the scarf you're wearing just because it's so pretty.

■ Do something to benefit someone else. When I was putting together my car seat mirrors, I hired people with disabilities to assemble them, through work training centers my husband is affiliated with. Providing work for them really made me happy. So does making a meal for a housebound friend, or paying the toll for the person behind me. Those random acts of kindness really create a lot of energy.

When I had an online baby store several years ago, I donated a percentage of every sale to a charity. I also gave actual products to an organization that distributed them to moms in need. To me, this is how the world works; it was a no-brainer.

AND NOW FOR THE FLIP SIDE

Our culture has encouraged us to produce relentlessly and it's burning everyone out. Even vacations become a kind of exhausting "have to"—how many people do you know who say they need to take a vacation to recover from their vacation? (And the ironic thing is that if you're doing work you really truly love, why would you want to take a vacation from it anyway?)

I can't stress this enough: regular periods of rest and relaxation—not "vacations," but restful times—are a necessity, and every inventor or creative person needs stretches of time to simply goof around, daydream, and

do nothing. It counts, because into those moments of not-doing, of still-ness, sometimes great ideas will arrive without any warning. So make sure you factor in guilt-free do-nothing days and love yourself for taking time to lie on the bed and read a good book or watch a silly movie once in a while.

When I reach a "block" (usually when I am trying to assemble a pro-totype), there are times when I just can't figure out a solution. This frus-trates me but it also challenges me. Because failure is not an option, instead of giving up, I practice positive thinking and I experiment until it works out. I just need to step away from it for a while—and then the an-swer comes to me. So be assured that those times of doing nothing can actually be the container for a fresh new idea or solution to come in, often when you least expect it. For more on hanging in there rather than giving up, see Chapter 8.

CHAPTER

7

Do You **N**ourish Your Dreams? Feed 'Em!

We grow great by dreams.

—WOODROW WILSON

The truth is that if you don't nourish your dreams and ideas, they'll die. Just as living things need to be fed, dreams and ideas need metaphorical food and water. Here's a poignant story from my own childhood to illustrate the point. I had a pet turtle that I kept in a cool plastic container with a little palm tree. Being young and stupid, I forgot to feed it—and was horrified to find the poor thing dead a few days later. Even after several decades, I still feel terrible. I learned the hard way that you have to take care of the things that are entrusted to you—and your creative ideas are just like that turtle: they depend on you for nourishment. How many of us have had a great inspiration but felt it fizzle out because we didn't pursue it or pay attention to it? It happens all the time.

THE BANQUET

It's not good enough for our dreams to exist in bare-survival mode, either—we want them to grow all shiny and strong. In the last chapter, we saw how important it is to foster positive habits of living, thinking, and being to encourage this. Now I offer a few ideas to continue the process. Because even though we—and our dreams—can subsist on bread and water, there's a whole banquet of things to enjoy when it comes to nourishing our dreams!

Before we go any further, a note about regular (or at least daily) meals: Just as the Muses (who inspire creative people of all kinds) like to be courted and honored regularly, so do our dreams respond to regular attention. The more consistently you take time to feed a dream, the more it will repay you. Set aside time every day to work on your project (and remember that time spent imagining and daydreaming counts!). It makes me feel so good inside when I know I'm moving in a forward direction—because I know I'm nourishing and growing my dream. I also know that if I neglect it, it will most likely wither and fade, and I don't want that to happen!

For me, early morning is the best time to feed my projects, but any time you can wrest away from kids, driving, work, and all the rest of the daily-living stuff is good. Dreams seem to prefer a set "mealtime," but they'll take anything they can get, as long as you give some time every day. The food metaphor really is a good one: some days we eat more than we do on others, but we do need to eat every day. Dreams, projects, ideas, and businesses need daily attention in order to thrive, just as we do.

Setting the Table

Some of us need to nourish our dreams at a desk in a studio or office—the equivalent of sitting down to a meal at a table with napkins and silverware. And if you have access to such a space, that's great! But I have a writer friend who runs another business as well, and part of his job requires driving people to and from stores, waiting while they shop. He drops them off, then gets his basket full of writing work from the trunk, sits reclined in the front seat, and works on it.

I can really relate to this idea of a metal-cubicle-on-wheels, since I've done a lot of work in my car over the years. When you add up all those minutes, it turns out that most of us spend hours of time a week simply waiting—to pick kids up from school or from a sports event or dance class. We wait in doctors' or dentists' offices, or in line at the grocery store, or in a dozen other places. I've learned that this waiting-around time can be used to nourish an idea or project; all I need is a pad of paper and a pencil, or, failing that, just my own mind! Any time can be a good time to pay some attention to your dream. And if you spend a lot of time driving, use the recording feature on your cell phone or invest in a recorder so you can capture any brilliant ideas you have without endangering yourself or others by reaching for a pen and paper.

The Menu

Here are a few tasty dishes that I've found helpful when it comes to nourishing my dreams:

■ If you're feeling hungry creatively, find a community that will feed you. Networking is so much easier to do in this age of the Internet; just find an interest group and join. LinkedIn is a great resource here (see Chapter 16 to learn more about social media).

■ Go to a workshop, seminar, or webinar. Learning something new is always nourishing and you never know how it will inform or help your project and ideas.

■ Watch a TED talk by a business owner or fellow inventor to get really juiced up! Go to www.ted.com for a listing of wonderful short talks that will appeal to anyone—and they're free.

■ Read biographies or autobiographies about or by people you admire. Remember, everyone starts out as an ordinary person, but some achieve greatness. I love to find out how real people did it! You may find it empowers you to feel you can do it, too.

■ Watch programs that inspire you. For me, it was the Roloff family on *Little People, Big World* that really lit me up. This is a reality TV show about a couple with dwarfism, working and raising their four kids. The parents are both highly successful in spite of their small stature and multiple medical issues. Matt, the father, has several businesses, and one was designing and manufacturing a special step stool for short people—an invention that solved a daily problem for him. Watching their business savvy and talent (the wife, Amy, is a teacher and public speaker) and the courage with which they dealt with their dwarfism and their lives made me admire them tremendously. Also, it made me feel like I had no excuse not to nourish my dreams when I've had it relatively easy in comparison!

■ Find a mentor—or be one. I work with college students who are studying entrepreneurship, and it nourishes me as well as them. I love passing on information that has helped me. That's why I wrote this book! And working with a real person who is a living example is a lot of fun.

■ Keep the bigger picture in mind. Whenever I have to make a decision in business or life, I always ask myself, "Is this in line with the kind of legacy I want my children to have?" It feeds me on such a deep level to know I'm creating a positive legacy for them.

■ Allow yourself to be inspired and nourished by the challenges presented to you by your loved ones. The truth is that without my kids, I wouldn't have needed to invent child-centered products. What a gift they are to me! They've allowed me to experience firsthand the satisfaction of filling a need, and they keep me trying my best to be a positive role model.

Preventing—and Curing—Indigestion

No "Overeating"

Be picky about what you put in your creative mouth, because if you eat what everyone else feeds you, you will end up filled with unoriginal, inauthentic ideas—and a bad case of indigestion. Learn to choose wisely by paying attention to what you need and keeping in mind that not every piece of delicious advice is good for you or your project. This even applies to the advice in this book: always run everything through the filter of your own good judgment.

Consider the case of the petting zoo. I often used to take my daughters to our local one, where there was a gumball machine filled with food pellets you could buy for 25 cents. People would buy handfuls and feed the animals all day long. Boy, were those goats, ducks, and pigs unhealthy!

They didn't know when to stop eating. And remember the girl in *Charlie and the Chocolate Factory* who chewed the blueberry gum and blew up like a huge blue beach ball? How we take in nourishment to feed our dreams and goals isn't that different: it's good to have a discerning palate when it comes to feeding your creative baby, so that your project will end up gleaming with creative muscle rather than being all puffed up with hot air or flab.

The Truth Statement Antacid

The Irish poet William Butler Yeats wrote, "Tread softly because you tread on my dreams." It is a terrible shame when they get trampled by other people! What's even worse is that a lot of the trampling often happens inside our own minds. I like to imagine that the negative self-talk I sometimes hear in my head belongs to a nasty troll with acid indigestion. Like the trolls in Scandinavian fairy tales, he's big and loutish and hairy and mean. He belongs to a part of me that doesn't like me very much. Why should I listen to him? And why would I want to spend time with people who basically share his attitude? Nobody needs to have their parade rained on, by other people or by your own troll voices. So the next time your troll starts telling you your ideas are worthless, or if you've been exposed to the acidic negativity of others that makes you feel less-than, try this antacid: make a Truth Statement.

First of all, a Truth Statement is not like New Agey affirmations that say things like "I am filled with light and love" when you really feel like biting the heads off rats. A Truth Statement starts with the truth and builds from there. Here are two examples:

"I got really hurt and upset when my friend said she thought my ambitions were unrealistic. Ouch. But I have to remember that she's not very happy in her own life and maybe she doesn't like to think I could do something that she can't."

"I got really depressed today thinking that I'll never amount to much, but I'm going take some time right now to remember all the things I've managed to do this week, and that will make me feel better."

There is something very liberating about telling yourself the real truth instead of sugarcoating—and then making the choice to think positively and to do something healing, self-loving, or useful as an antidote.

All of us can partake in the feast of the inventor's life and grow healthy, self-sustaining projects that will eventually take their place at the table for the good of all. I know I'm enjoying every morsel of the meal; seeing my creative ideas take on a vital life of their own is one of the most satisfying feelings I've ever known.

Got **T**enacity?
Hang In and Hang On!

Many of life's failures are people who did not realize how close they were to success when they gave up.

—THOMAS A. EDISON

All the imagination and skill in the world won't get us where we need to go if we're quitters. Just as you can't sit down at a piano the first time and play like a pro, it's unusual (to say the least) for success to fall into our laps immediately. In order to make our dreams come true, we need staying power. We need to learn how to pace ourselves. We need to take pleasure in the process rather than focusing solely on outcomes. And we need to practice radical self-belief so that when the going gets tough, we hang tough. That's precisely when it's most important for us to live up to the best in ourselves, believe in ourselves, and do what we can to bring our success closer to fruition.

A WORD ABOUT FLEXIBILITY

Keep in mind that, while it's essential to remain determined, we also have to be willing to change. If I had stuck to every detail of my original ideas, they never would have been successful. I had to adapt, take helpful criticism into account, and change my plan when needed. So, while I was ferociously committed to getting my products in thousands of retail stores, I wasn't invested in the details on how they would get there, or exactly what they'd look like when they did. Those details were completely flexible. In other words, the best attitude to cultivate is a winning combination of self-belief and tenacity, and the wisdom to see where we may need to adjust.

My usual rule is, if I hear the same—or a very similar—piece of constructive criticism from more than one source, I might start to listen to it and reset my plans accordingly. I've learned the hard way that there is a big difference between tenacity and pig-headed stubbornness.

WORDS TO LIVE BY

Nobody gives up when things are going well (unless you have a Cinderella complex, but that's the subject of another book). Nope, it's when things don't work out or we face crushing disappointments that we're tempted to throw in the towel. So here are some affirmations and personal stories to help you keep the faith and stay the course.

Mottoes and Mantras

Your new motto needs to be, "I can learn from this." If your idea doesn't float someone's boat, that person wasn't the right one to help you bring your product to the market. Keep refining your idea and trying to put it out there until you find the person who *is* right. Keep going, searching, learning.

And how about this for a mantra? "Trust your gut." After looking at the statistics, one patent attorney told me that the odds were not great that I would ever get a patent. He advised me not to go forward—but when I did, I got that patent and several subsequent patents, too. Which just goes to show that you can't always trust the statistics.

Inspiring Quotes

Never underestimate the power of a quote that puts something important into the perfect words. Read these whenever you need a quick shot of encouragement for hanging in there.

When the world says, "Give up," Hope whispers, "Try it one more time."
—AUTHOR UNKNOWN

Fall seven times, stand up eight.
—JAPANESE PROVERB

It's not that I'm so smart, it's just that I stay with problems longer.
—ALBERT EINSTEIN

Life isn't about finding yourself. Life is about creating yourself.

—GEORGE BERNARD SHAW

They can because they think they can.

—VIRGIL

Your success and happiness lies in you.

—HELEN KELLER

Perseverance will accomplish all things.

—AMERICAN PROVERB

Don't be discouraged. It's often the last key in the bunch that opens the lock.

—AUTHOR UNKNOWN

If you fell down yesterday, stand up today.

—H. G. WELLS

Most people never run far enough on their first wind to find out they've got a second.

—WILLIAM JAMES

Never confuse a single defeat with a final defeat.

—F. SCOTT FITZGERALD

Water is fluid, soft and yielding. But water will wear away rock,
which is rigid and cannot yield . . . what is soft is strong.

—LAO TZU

The history of the world is full of men who rose to leadership by
sheer force of self-confidence, bravery, and tenacity.
—MAHATMA GANDHI

Luck is tenacity of purpose.
—ELBERT HUBBARD

I know of no such unquestionable badge and ensign of a sovereign mind
as that of tenacity of purpose.
—RALPH WALDO EMERSON

Courage is not having the strength to go on;
it is going on when you don't have the strength.
—TEDDY ROOSEVELT

Patient persistence pierces through indifference.
—PROVERBS 25:15

Never give up, no matter what is going on around you. Never give up.
—THE FOURTEENTH DALAI LAMA

Let me tell you the secret that has led me to my goal.
My strength lies solely in my tenacity.
—LOUIS PASTEUR

Paralyze resistance with persistence.
—WOODY HAYES

TRUST YOUR JOURNEY—AND YOUR PLAN

Trust that things will work out for the best *if you keep trying*. You may need to change your approach or your mind, or refine your idea, but if you refuse to give up, you will eventually reach a goal. Or three!

I could have packed it in at so many stages of the game. One company that was on the verge of signing a license agreement with me changed their marketing plan at the last minute and the whole deal fell through. I could have said, "To heck with it" then and there, but I kept at it—and a year later another licensee approached me. Another example: a European distributor that I met at a trade show wanted a product of mine and I paid a lawyer to draft an agreement. After weeks of back-and-forth it fizzled out. But instead of throwing in the towel, I spent months making cold calls and following them up until finally things panned out.

Once my original design for the car seat mirror was out and selling well, I wanted to stay ahead of the competition and patent every option for rear-facing car seat mirrors that I could think of. But a patent attorney I consulted told me I shouldn't be my own competition. He counseled me to give up, but my intuition said to plow forward. Good thing I did, too: I got in ahead of other companies that would have jumped on the booming mirror business. And I got every patent that I applied for.

BE LIKE AN OWL

Owls have turned something that is a disadvantage—darkness—into an advantage: when most predators are asleep, owls take the field. They're also known for their ability to turn their heads around nearly 360 degrees. So let the owl be your guide; when you're seemingly at an impasse, try looking at it a different way. And, when you can, turn what seems like a disadvantage into an advantage. At one time I developed a safety mirror for use on baby backpacks and pitched it to a well-known outdoor store. That company declined with thanks—but I noticed a year later that it had incorporated a mirror into its new line of backpacks! This could have been a terrible blow (and a perfect excuse to abandon hope), but instead I sold the mirrors to people with older-model backpacks.

The world is full of great stories from famous and successful people who had to surmount obstacle after obstacle with their sheer fighting spirit. I met Debbi Fields (of Mrs. Fields Cookies) at a trade show where she was the keynote speaker. She told us about all the roadblocks she had encountered, from food manufacturers who wouldn't sell her ingredients because she wanted small quantities at first, to family members who were used to formal business plans, to banks that refused to fund her. She was even told by a market research company that her cookies would never sell because people wanted crunchy ones, not soft ones! But even after all those years, her passion and stick-to-itiveness were palpable, and that was what finally persuaded others to help her. There was the great guy who sold her the quality chocolate she needed from his car because the quantities weren't enough for his truck . . . and the banker who did say yes, because he believed in her and her enthusiasm. He took a huge risk on a business model that had never been done before, but it worked out, and he handled her accounts for years. Everywhere she turned, someone was giving her a reason to quit, but she just refused. That kind of tenacity—along with great cookies—made her the success she is today. But if you think you have to be a mean, fierce pit bull to make it, think again: Mrs. Fields is the kindest, nicest person you'd ever want to meet!

EXERCISES TO TRY

Tempted to just give up? Try these exercises first.

The Encouraging Letter. When you're at the breaking point, it can help to get some encouragement—and you're the best person to get it from, because who knows you better than you do? So, write yourself a letter. Remind yourself of your dearest and most cherished dreams. Enumerate all the things you've managed to accomplish. Tell yourself to persevere. Then put it in an envelope with a stamp and mail it to yourself. After it has arrived and you've read it, keep it in a special, safe place. It can be wonderful to re-read these letters after you've accomplished some of your goals.

The Courage Bowl. Write a list of things that make you believe in yourself and want to keep going. Cut the list into pieces and fold each of them up, then put them all in a special bowl. Whenever you need a reminder that you and your dreams are worth believing in, pick a piece of paper at random and read it. Put it by your computer or on your bathroom mirror or carry it in your pocket. You could also do this with several of the inspiring quotes listed earlier in this chapter, or with others that you find yourself. The Internet is a fabulous resource for quotes.

Reasons Why. Without overthinking, write down at least three reasons why your idea has merit; how it would be useful or helpful. Reread this list whenever you're ready to quit to remind yourself that the world would lose out on these benefits if you give up.

As my dad would say of people with no follow-through, "He's a fiddler. He'll never be a violin player." What we want is to give our ideas the very best of ourselves, and to believe enough in them that we'll go the distance, do what needs to be done, refuse to give up, and keep the faith. We all can be violin players!

The Six Simple Steps to Invention

What They Are and How to Use Them

You don't have to see the whole staircase, just take the first step.

—MARTIN LUTHER KING, JR.

Now you've learned how to develop the traits shared by most great inventors, so you can do what it takes to be a successful one. And there has never been a better time to make money from your ideas than right now. Why? Because:

➤ Inventors are in the mainstream. It's cool to be one.

➤ There are multiple TV shows highlighting inventors.

➤ You can file for a provisional patent that will protect your idea rather than having to go the whole-hog patent route—and it will make sure you're the one to get that all-important first-to-file date.

➤ Colleges and universities have entrepreneurship programs.

➤ Companies big and small are searching for, or open to, outside ideas.

➤ Sleazeball companies that purport to help inventors are evaporating, or at least being called to account.

➤ There are plenty of crowdfunding and angel investor opportunities available.

➤ With the Internet, there is free research at your fingertips.

➤ It's easier than it ever was to reach decision makers.

➤ Social media networks and marketing are a huge advantage.

➤ Prototype and printing methods have never been cheaper or easier.

➤ And you have this book to guide you!

So—now it's time to learn the nuts and bolts of getting an idea to the marketplace. None of us are born knowing how to do it. In fact, when I started inventing products and building businesses around them 23 years ago, I had no clue how to get an idea from my notebook to store shelves. When I started out, there was no all-inclusive handbook I could turn to. I didn't know what options existed, who to ask, what a license was, whether or not I needed legal or accounting advice, how to protect or build my product. I was such a newbie! But I was determined to figure it out. And I did.

The good news is that I did all the legwork for you so you don't have to reinvent the wheel; it's all right here in this book. After all, the process can seem overwhelming if you're not familiar with it, which is why I've broken down the whole thing into six very doable steps.

Now, I've noticed that inventors who've made any money at all on their ideas try to teach, sell, or write a book about their method, as if they've discovered the secret sauce for success. But everyone's journey to success is different, and there is no one-size-fits-all way to make a million, even though people want to believe there is. Instead, this book offers you techniques for strengthening the six traits that will help you succeed, and the six steps that will help you reach your goals, along with a sense of the options you have. You do have options!

Most inventors, including me when I first started, are so inexperienced—and so excited about their idea—that they are willing to pay a company whatever it takes to help them get from concept to market. They want to pass the football and let somebody else carry it to the end zone. Based on the fact that I couldn't find any such company anywhere that didn't expect a huge up-front fee, and because I didn't have a ton of money to waste, I realized that I had to make my own game plan if I wanted to score a touchdown.

In this game, just because you write a check to somebody else does not guarantee better results. My advice is for *you* to put the effort in instead of hiring a middle person. And you have the advantage of my 6 + 6 steps so you can reap all the benefits of a successful product yourself—and save money in the process.

Whenever people find out I'm an inventor, nine times out of ten they get very excited and want to tell me their idea. I have to stop them right there because it's never good to divulge your ideas to anybody until they're protected—and then they offer to give me half of their profits if I can get their product into stores! So many of them tell me that they're scared of people stealing their idea and they'd love to get their product out there but they don't have a clue how to proceed.

Most people will pay anybody who claims to be able to help them. Take the case of the guy whose booth was next to mine at a recent trade show. He told me he had just paid some outfit $10,000 to get him a patent. Well, it turns out that the company had applied for a provisional patent—and I felt really bad for him because I know that applying for a provisional patent only costs a little over $100. Can you believe it? What a gigantic rip-off. And the world is full of scammers like that. When I told the poor man how badly he'd been conned, he begged me to help him. I told him the steps he needed to take and he was so grateful. They're the same six steps you're about to discover. I want to prevent travesties like that $10,000 rip-off, and empower people to move forward on their own.

In the following chapters you'll be getting to know the six simple steps to invention. Think of them as a strategic blueprint for taking an idea and manifesting it into a thriving business. And in certain cases, you don't even have to do all of them! Your path to success will be as individual as you are.

Step One: Think It—It All Starts in Your Head. Every invention started with an idea, so the first step is coming up with one. You'll learn my techniques for getting the creative juices flowing: identify a need, solve a problem, and come up with the next hot thing.

Step Two: Cook It—Now Get Real. I'll show you how to determine whether your product is marketable, priced right, and has a potential for making a profit. I'll tell you what a sell sheet is and how to make one. Is your idea functional? Will it sell? What would your prototype look like? Get out the cardboard and duct tape and make a sample, then try my powerful technique of placing it on the shelf of your favorite store so you can begin to see it selling there.

Step Three: Protect It—Keep Thieves Away. I'll demystify the process of keeping your idea safe from the pirates that might try to scuttle your ship. Navigating the channels of protecting your product can be challenging, but I'll guide you through those shark-infested waters, showing you all the options of different types of protection, from a non-disclosure agreement (NDA), which can be free, to a provisional patent application (PPA), which costs a little over $100, to a full, or nonprovisional patent, which usually means going through a patent attorney, which costs money but is well worth it. But in some cases, you don't even necessarily need a patent at all.

Step Four: Pitch It—Make 'Em Want It Bad. Find out how to generate excitement for your product by implementing social media (once your idea is protected), finding out how to snag store buyers, take tradeshow shortcuts, and much more.

Step Five: Make It—Factory in the Kitchen (Or Not). Should you assemble your product yourself or find a licensed manufacturer? You may want to be the idea person, with somebody else taking the financial risk, or you may want to build an empire on your product. I'll help you figure it out. The variables are different for every product, but I'll cut to the chase so you can see which approach will work best for you and your idea.

Step Six: Bedazzle It—Add Bells and Whistles. Call them bells and whistles or added enhancements—when you add dazzle, buyers will be hot for your product. Learn to think like a buyer so your product will have the shelf life and attraction value it needs to keep selling for years to come.

So, let's start with Step One: How many inventors does it take to screw in a light bulb? The answer is one—and that's you. Turn the page and find out how.

CHAPTER

10

Think It (Step One)

It All Starts in Your Head

The mind is not a vessel to be filled but a fire to be kindled.

—PLUTARCH

Here's an inspiring thought: any manufactured product that now exists was once a mere gleam in someone's imagination. Before it could be a real thing, somebody had to come up with the idea. When you come to think about it, that's pretty empowering, because if they could do it, so can you. Where do ideas come from, anyway? Do they float around in the ether waiting for us to open our minds so they can zoom in like homing pigeons? What if we get tired of sitting around waiting for the brilliant idea to descend? How can we be more proactive and snatch it out of the air instead? What can we do to get the Good Idea Fairy to visit us more often? Should we start making offerings or leaving bowls of milk on the

windowsill? We all want to come up with the next great idea. So how do we do that?

There were a lot of helpful hints in Chapter 3 to get you reading and noticing and becoming more awake, aware, and curious about life, and those are all good answers to the question. Now let's look at another answer.

START WITH WHAT YOU KNOW—BUT THINK OUTSIDE THE BOX

It's actually a brilliant approach to look around our everyday lives to see what we need, to notice what might come in handy or what would improve our lives or make things easier for us. As the ancient fabelist Aesop said, necessity is the mother of invention. In other words, the need for something is the very thing that will push you to create it.

Think of a few of the items we use every day. Some of us can't imagine life without them now, but sixty years ago they were unheard-of, or they existed in a much different, less evolved form. It's important to remember that so many inventions are variations on things that already exist—because everyone wants something newer, better, faster. One thing technology does is invite innovation and more versions of the same product. So think of things like cordless drills, dental floss, bagless vacuum cleaners, hands-free headsets, memory foam mattresses, teeth whiteners, fleece outerwear—the list could go on and on, not to mention the big things like computers and MP3 players and cell phones with built-in video cameras. Who could even have imagined some of this stuff? But somebody did. It gets you wondering about all the things that haven't been thought of yet. What can you imagine right now?

Most of us are in a kind of cultural fog, where what we see is all there is, but accessing the imagination creatively is what brings new things to life. It can all start with your identifying a need—and then figuring out a way to meet it. I know that's what worked for me.

You've already heard about what motivated me to invent the rear-facing car seat mirror, but it didn't stop there. Really, having children turned me into an inventing machine! Within an eight-month period, I also came up with several other new ideas, including the backpack safety mirror, which I mentioned in Chapter 8. I designed it for those times when I was carrying the baby in a backpack and I couldn't see whether she was asleep or if her little head was at a weird angle or whatever. It was sort of a logical extension of the car seat mirror, and it was easy for me to do, since by then I'd already figured out where to get mirrors. I did concentrate on just one invention at a time, though, because it's seldom good to be spread out all over the place. You'll usually get better results if you focus on one thing at a time. As the proverb says, if you chase two rabbits, you will lose them both.

When new cars came out with mandatory LATCH (Lower Anchors and Tethers for Children) systems to better secure car seats, the tether hook on the top became the perfect place to attach a car seat mirror, so I got a new patent to protect that method. Headrests were also featured in new cars, so I made that an option for attaching the mirrors as well.

Then there was the invention prompted by pain. When I carried my little ones in the backpack they would get bored and start looking for something to play with, and they grabbed my hair and earrings one too many times. If you have babies, you know they have a grip like a vise—yowch! I was inspired by those activity centers that you hang over a crib, so I fitted out a flap with lots of fun dangling stuff for little hands to grasp and play with—and it attached to the back of any hat. Voila—the Hat Wrap, a backpack entertainer that gives babies an enthralling source of fun and keeps parents pain-free. All of my kids loved it, especially my youngest, Meghan, who spent a lot of time in the backpack because the others had graduated to strollers or walking. That product was chosen one of the top ten products at a trade show and was featured on a major television show, during which the host wore one.

Once my children outgrew car seats, I designed a side door organizer for kids—because a child who is buckled in the backseat can't reach the toys or books or whatever is in the conventional backseat organizers, which were designed for older kids with longer arms. My organizer hooks onto the side door right next to the child and incorporates a collapsible drink holder and snack tray.

And of course I'm still at it. My family goes camping every summer, and making s'mores is a favorite activity. Trouble is, somebody was always getting too close to the campfire (once, my husband even fell in!), so I started playing with an idea for a retractable skewer and made a prototype. A little in-store research showed me that somebody had already thought of this, but someday I may try doing a variation on it, and I have other ideas around camping that I'm going to pursue as well.

Just recently, we were having dinner out and a waitress tipped her tray and everything on it slid, accidentally spilled scalding chowder on my daughter. Thank goodness Taylor was okay (she was cold and wearing her heavy fleece jacket, which protected her) but it got me thinking about designing a safer tray so this will never happen to anyone else.

And after watching a show about Japanese warriors, I noticed the sword being pulled out of its sheath and suddenly a light bulb went off in my head: why can't kitchen knife holders have built-in sharpeners so every time you pull one out it gets sharpened? I'm a big fan of dual-purpose products and this fit the bill, so I general-searched it. I found out that a form of it already exists, but I have something up my sleeve as a variation of this that I may pursue someday. This gives you some idea of how your mind can stay perennially engaged as an inventor: everything is grist for the mill. As you get better and better at coming up with new ideas, you'll begin to realize which ones are most worthy of your time, energy, and attention. I'll tell you more about marketability (which will help you make those decisions!) in Chapter 11. As you get the hang of the process, you will be able to tackle more than one project at a time.

Try this fun exercise:

Walk into your kitchen with a pad of paper and a pen and make a quick list of ten things you see there that you use every day. Now sit down with your list and think about how each of these could be changed, varied, combined, or improved. Feel free to be as imaginative as you like! For instance, how many times have I poured boiling water into my plastic drip-filter holder only to have it overflow? Well, somebody came up with a design that has holes around the bottom so you can see when your mug is full. And I just read about beer glasses that have laser etchings on the inside bottom to create bubbles for constant aroma release. What can you imagine?

As you can see, every aspect of your life offers problems to solve, and potential inventions to solve them. I'm a dog owner as well as a parent, and like all dog owners, I was faced with the perennial problem of picking up and disposing of solid waste when I took Coconut for her daily walks. Eww. Dog poop has fairly recently been labeled a hazardous substance and you get hefty fines now for not picking it up. After a particularly messy poop-bag disaster, I came up with a nifty, neat solution to that, too, called Parachute Dog waste bags, but I'll tell you more about

73

that in Chapter 16. (Believe me, if I can make money with dog poop, you can make money with just about anything!) Just remember that as both laws and technology change, they give you lots of opportunities to jump on a wave and surf it!

But Don't Stop There

You don't necessarily have to be an expert at something to see where improvement or change might be possible. Take Google, for example. That giant company has a "20 percent time" program allowing employees to go outside their usual area of expertise and develop other technologies for 20 percent of their work week—which translates to taking a full day every week to explore other ventures. The result? Lots of new products that were once someone's 20-percent project.

So, while it's great to mine the needs around us in our daily lives for ideas, you can also strengthen your peripheral vision.

A Few Things to Keep in Mind

As you think and explore and imagine the possibilities for new products, remember:

➤ *It needs to have pizzazz.* When buyers see your product, they need to think "Wow, what a great idea! Why didn't I think of that?"

➤ *It should have broad appeal.* If only one or two people want or need this, it won't go anywhere. Tap in to the group mind and come up with things that would benefit many people.

➤ *Keep it simple.* Simple ideas mean easier and less complicated proto-type and manufacturing processes. It also means that the product may be cheaper to make, and less expensive to buy.

➤ *Think refills.* You might as well imagine a product that people need a lot of, or that needs constant refilling—like razor blades or printer cartridges or water purifier filters. Constant refills mean a constant income flow.

➤ *Let existing products morph in your mind.* Just as my Hat Wrap was a transformation of those great mobile activity bars that hang over a crib, you can train yourself to see the possibilities in almost any product you run across.

➤ *Consider dual purpose; two-in-one is good.* Many people use my Para-chute Dog waste bags as portable food and water bowls for hikes or long walks, and the Hat Wrap protects hair and jewelry as well as giving your baby something to play with. And since step-saving and space-saving are important to people, think of combining products. For instance, a cake slicer/server means one utensil instead of two, so your junk drawer is less cluttered. Here are some other examples: ice scraper/snow brush, spork (instead of a spoon and fork), tooth-brush with a dental pick on the end, lipstick-and-mirror in one. A woman I met at a recent trade show had come up with an ingenious product: a headband/reading glasses combo that keeps your hair off your face and keeps your glasses handy, while doing away with those little chain-around-your-neck things.

➤ *Know why people buy.* Since you want people to buy your idea or product, it helps to know what motivates people to buy things in the first place. First of all, buying is emotional. Even in a bad economy, people buy—to feel powerful, safe, better about them-

selves. They want products that save time and are convenient, and they also want what's new and exciting. Packaging is key: the right packaging can be very seductive and a great place to express your brand (see more about branding in Chapter 16). A friend told me that, even though she has a set of plastic measuring cups, and a set of metal ones, she was so enamored of a ceramic set marketed under the name of a famous cooking show host that she had to have them—and it was the pretty packaging that convinced her. Some people want to buy things that make them feel like one of the crowd, while others want products that express their individuality. And people like things that are packaged for a specific purpose. But basically, we buy to improve our lives and make ourselves happier.

Scout a Store

So, here's a way to start practicing. Go to a local store—a large one, preferably—and pick an aisle, any aisle. Cruise the products, looking at them as an inventor, not a consumer. Take notes: What improvements can you think of? How could these products be repurposed? Say you're in the bath section. Can anything you see there be used in a different room in the house? Someone I know once bought a pretty stoneware toothbrush holder to keep her desk pencils and pens in. If the design could be tweaked, this idea could be marketed to an entirely different audience: stationery stores, office suppliers, upscale catalogs, and houseware stores—you could tap into a whole new set of buyers or licensees. Could any products be combined to make one thing out of two? Do any of them inspire you to come up with something entirely new?

Organize Your Ideas

Until very recently, whoever could prove they came up with a product idea first got the patent, so everyone had to keep detailed journals and logs of their thought processes so they could show they had the brainstorm before the other guy. It's different now: whoever files first gets the patent. But it's still important to stay organized, just in case you need to prove something later. Here's how:

Keep detailed notes. Because I always have my cell phone with me when I'm out, I enter my notes in it—every time I identify a need, into the phone it goes. Then, once I get home, I transcribe my notes into my notebooks and mull over possible fixes for the needs or issues I identified. Believe me, I've got lots and lots of notebooks! I recommend using bound ones, so it's difficult to tear the pages out, and I number those pages and date my entries. You can buy cheap composition books at the dollar store.

Try visually mapping your ideas. Visuals are important for me, and they may be for you, as well. I like to use a technique that can help you visualize your ideas and get them down on paper in an organized, clear, and interesting way. Rather than full sentences, visual mapping uses words or phrases. You start with a central idea or issue in the middle of the page and then branch out from there, drawing a line from the central idea outward for each related thought that comes to mind, writing down the thought at the end of each line and making connections as you go.

Don't be afraid to do rough, messy sketches. Even if you think you can't draw, it can be fun to do quick scribbly sketches to see what your idea would be like if it were a reality. It can be helpful to use graph paper to keep your lines straight.

A FEW WORDS OF WARNING

Just remember, although your ideas are precious, you don't need to go running to a patent office for a full-on nonprovisional patent at this point. You may not even have to go through all the hassle of getting a full-on patent or starting a business, either; you can make money by renting your ideas to a company (licensing) and I'll show you how in Chapter 11. Meanwhile, until you're protected (and I'll show you how to keep people from stealing your ideas in Chapter 12), remember:

■ Keep your ideas to yourself. This means tell nobody, except your significant other. Maybe.

■ In general, avoid companies that purport to help inventors. Many of them want substantial up-front money. Although some are safer than others, it makes more sense to do the work yourself and not take a chance. Many such outfits are shameless scams, but because there is such general ignorance of the patent process and because most people have very little time to pursue making money with their ideas themselves, inventors can often fall prey to hucksters who promise the world and deliver exactly nothing. Unless you're an attorney and speak fluent legalese, the fine print of any agreement is usually a mystery. It's meant to be. I just heard the story of a well-known actor who sent his invention idea off to a company that stole it out from under him, and he won't see a penny from it. In Chapter 14 I'll tell you more about the different kinds of companies that say they will help inventors obtain a patent and/or get a product into the market. But for now, just remember that even reputable and reasonably priced places still require you to sign an agreement that you might not like if you could understand the deal.

■ With my help, you can figure all of this out, save money, and keep your idea safe. You're smarter than you think!

Now the light bulbs are popping on over your head and that's great: a brilliant idea is a beautiful thing. But before you can sell it, you need to Cook It, so turn on your burners and get real!

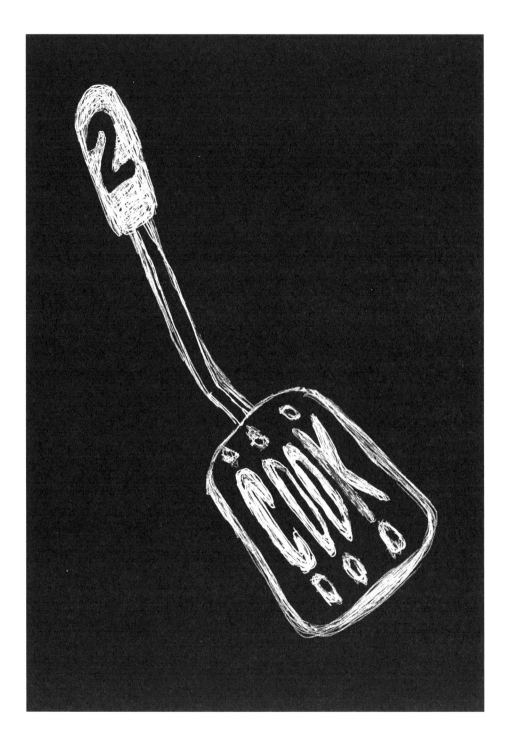

Cook It (Step Two)

Now Get Real

It's all theory until you see for yourself whether or not something works.

—JULIA CHILD

Now it's time to get serious about your idea. This chapter will give you the tools to bring it into tangible form—because unless we go to the next step, it will stay in the realm of imagination and the world will miss out on the benefits of the dream-product we can see so clearly. And it's such a fun part of the process!

I called this chapter "Cook It" for two reasons. First, you'll be taking the ingredients of your idea and cooking them into something real. Second, to bring your idea to market you need to tend several pots at once, sort of like cooking a Thanksgiving dinner or hosting a dinner party. But you can do it! Just turn on the burners and think of the feast you're producing. It's so important to prove to yourself and to the world that your idea is a valuable

and functioning product. Always remember that you're the head chef here, and you're in control.

Here are the how-to instructions:

DEFINE YOUR IDEA

Time to get very specific here. What do you want your product to do? What need does it fill? What do you want it to look like? Why is it important? What benefits will it offer? You need to have a fairly detailed idea of what you want to do before you can go on to the next important steps—sort of like needing to know what meal you want to cook before you go shopping for ingredients.

I like to do some preliminary research that will tell me if I should pursue my idea at all, before I go charging off to the attorney. Research will be useful for you, too. If your research suggests you should move forward and you want patent protection, you will visit your attorney armed with information and knowledge that will save you time and money. My own patent attorney has told me that he likes it when clients come in with this preliminary research already done, since it helps him understand the goals of the inventor and how the invention works—and it makes his job all that much easier. Potential licensees will also appreciate any data you find, especially if it shows the differences between your idea and others.

DO YOUR RESEARCH

Once you have a clear idea about your product, one strategy may be to go ahead and file for a provisional patent application (see Chapter 12), since the new first-to-file law will reward that kind of forward thinking. Even if it turns out that somebody has already thought of your idea, you're only out a little over $100, and some of you might find it's worth it to be the first to file. But it can also be helpful to do some research. Why? Six reasons:

1. *To know if it's already selling and who your competition is.* For starters, pretend you're a customer looking online for your product, go to Google, type in search words, and then click on "images." You'll get a visual overview of the products out there. This will tell you if there is already something like your idea on the market. To use one of my own inventions as an example, I'd type in "car mirrors," "car seat mirrors," "baby mirrors," "rear-facing car seat mirrors," or "car seat accessories." Use any combination of relevant words you can think of. Then take a close look at the products, if any, that come up to see what others have done, making a note of details that will be useful to you as you compare your product with theirs:

> Product name
> Price range from low to high
> Materials used
> What the product claims to do
> Packaging (box, plastic bag with header, hanger tag, etc.)
> Manufacturer

After you've done your online research, go to stores and do the same kind of sleuthing; the merchandise taking up space on the shelves is a terrific source of information. Always take a notepad and pen with you, and when you find a product that is similar to yours, make the same kinds of notes that you did online, also checking for patent numbers. If there is no similar product, you can look for products that complement your idea, because your product may be a nice extension of someone's line. For instance, there were no car seat mirrors at the time, so I noted car seat accessories and travel items, since I figured that was where my product would belong. Snap a photo with your phone, while you're at it. This information will come in handy, and you'll see why later on in this chapter.

2. *To minimize risk.* You don't want to infringe on an existing patent, because if somebody got there first, and you try to steal their thunder, you could have a nasty lawsuit on your hands. That means you'll need to search to see if your idea has been patented already. And it's not enough to say, "Well, I didn't see it in any stores so I think I'm okay," because not all patents have been made into products. In fact, most of them haven't. Just because you don't see it in the store doesn't mean there's not a patent on it.

You can do most of your research online. If you want to learn about patents in general, go to www.uspto.gov. It's a really good resource for learning about all aspects of intellectual property. To search for existing patents that may be like your idea, go to www.google.com/patents, which is really easy to use: type in a few general search words that could apply to your product, and see what comes up.

Be sure to look at the drawings/images section of each patent to see if it looks similar to your idea. If something does, proceed to the claims section and read what the inventor is claiming about their product. Does it do everything yours will do?

But even if you do find a patent that is similar to your idea, don't freak out, especially if it isn't a product in a store yet: it can look like yours but the wording of a patent can make all the difference and/or you may be able to vary your idea enough to avoid infringement and warrant a different patent (more about that in Chapter 12). You can get a patent attorney's opinion. In fact, you could have the attorney do the whole search, but that can get pretty expensive, which is why I advise you to do as much of the legwork yourself as you possibly can. The more homework you do, the more money you'll save.

What's a Patent Attorney?

Don't make the mistake of assuming that a regular attorney can handle your patent concerns, no matter what she or he tells you. Patent attorneys are specialists in patent law. Only patent attorneys and patent agents are licensed to practice before the United States Patent and Trademark Office (USPTO). I'll tell you how to find a patent attorney in the next chapter. And while we're talking about the law, please remember that I'm not a lawyer. These are suggestions that have worked for me, but to be really safe, you should consult with a patent attorney.

3. *To see if there's interest.* Research can also include asking potential customers what they think of your concept in general terms. Be cagey and don't tell them it's your idea, and don't give away any details. At this point you should just want to see if there is general interest and gather whatever

comments are offered. Remember that friends and family aren't objective enough to offer the most valuable opinions—and they're probably not the proper end users for your product anyway. And be sure to take only the most valuable feedback to heart.

If you want to get specific advice from someone, be sure to have that person sign a non-disclosure agreement (NDA) before you reveal any details. You can run your idea by small-store buyers or salespersons for more feedback (with a signed NDA), or put a survey online in your social networks or on your website or send it out as e-mail (see Chapter 16). But remember that your idea is not protected yet, so be very, very general. I used a survey on my website about existing dog waste disposal systems and got some very useful feedback about the benefits that people wanted and the improvements they wanted to see.

When asked, "What bothers you most about existing waste bags?" 42 percent said carrying the full bag, 27 percent said difficult to open, 18 percent said tying a knot, 10 percent said running out, and 3 percent said storing bags at home. This information confirmed that my system worked better than anything currently on the market—without giving any of my ideas away.

What's an NDA?

It's a legal document called a non-disclosure agreement. This is a mutual agreement between two parties stating that all the information will be kept confidential. You and the other person both sign and retain an original copy. You will learn more about this in Chapter 12.

4. *To start thinking about price.* As you look at the range of prices among your competitors, you can start to determine your own MSRP (which stands for manufacturer's suggested retail price). It's useful to study the lowest and highest prices of items that are similar to yours and then put your pricing somewhere in between—as long as your product is made from similar materials, with nothing unusual. If you're envisioning a deluxe model, price it higher. I usually set my price first, and then figure out how to make the item come in at a cost that will work. If there are no similar products, you can come up with your MSRP by costing out your actual materials.

5. *To find potential licensees.* Every product you find that is similar to yours or would be a good fit with yours is a treasure trove, because printed right there, whether on the item or in copy you found online, is the name of the manufacturer. This is your free list of potential licensees. There are online sites that want you to pay big bucks for lists like this, but why pay for something when you can get it free? Plus, a lot of online sites send you outdated lists containing names of companies that have gone out of business. By doing the research yourself you can be sure your information is current. So make sure you use that notepad you always travel with to jot everything down, or take close-up photos of those packages with your phone. (I call my iPhone my inventorPhone because it has everything I need—calendar, world clock, calculator, voice recorder, camera, video, and notepad. And I can research online with it and even order and pay for my coffee with an app.) Then you can start a typed list of potential licensees when you get home.

What's a Licensee?

A licensee is a company that agrees to manufacture and sell your product or idea, and in return they send you payments, usually in the form of royalties. In other words, licensees do all the work of production, marketing, shipping, assuming liability, etc. for you—and then they send you money. This is the perfect plan for inventors because it may sidestep the cost of getting a full patent and/or starting your own business around your idea. Not all of us are meant to be full-blown entrepreneurs, but our ideas still need to get out there.

6. *To gather vital details for your sell sheet.* Now you've taken a good look at the competition. What benefits does your idea offer that the others don't? Is it faster, easier to use, sleeker, better? Does it do more great stuff? Or is it new and completely original? When you learn how to make a sell sheet, you'll be whittling all these benefits down into a one-sentence statement that serves as a magic hook to attract buyers or licensees.

What if your research reveals that somebody already holds a patent on what you want to do and it's selling in stores and there's no way you could do it better? I know you're disappointed, but try to detach and think of your research as a blessing that kept you from wasting time and money. Then jump right into your next idea. If you need a refresher, go back and reread Chapter 4.

Remember, if your research shows a patent that looks like your idea but there is no product in the stores yet, you can be the first to market if your version is different enough. You can also think about buying the patent that already exists or designing around the existing patent. Here's where the patent attorney can help, since it's well worth the cost of hiring one to find out whether or not your product constitutes infringement. I always listen to my attorney when it comes to infringement issues. However, marketability is a different matter. Keep in mind the story about my former patent attorney, who advised me not to go forward based on the results of his research. While I respected him for not just taking my money and running with it when he didn't think the statistics were good for patenting my product, I ignored him, went ahead with the project because I just knew it was marketable despite those statistics, got the patent, and did really well with it. Just saying.

What's a Sell Sheet?

It's a simple one-page description designed to entice licensees, buyers, or tradeshow attendees and get them fired up over your product. You'll learn how to create one later in this chapter.

If your research comes up with no matching patent and no matching product in stores—congratulations! Now you're ready for the next step.

MAKE A PROTOTYPE

The process of making prototypes really isn't that different from the stuff we did when we were kids. Remember making toys out of anything we could lay our grubby little hands on? "Telephones" out of string and tin cans, kazoos out of combs and tissue paper, whistles out of blades of grass, spitball launchers from ballpoint pens or drinking straws—the list goes on and on.

I recommend making a prototype of your product because the process is hugely instructive, but you don't always absolutely have to make one.

When Not to Make a Prototype

If your product is too expensive or complicated, you can always pitch it using a professional-looking illustration or a photoshopped photo. That said, if you're seeking funding, your sources will probably require a working prototype.

I love making prototypes so much that my final versions usually end up being my actual products!

Why Prototypes Are Useful

➤ A good prototype will prove that your idea functions. For instance, I tested the strength of the attachment system on my first mirror by affixing it to the fabric on my rocking chair and then violently rocking it back and forth to make sure it wouldn't fall off. And it didn't! (I knew my licensee would do actual crash-testing that I couldn't afford, but this was a great start.) It's also really handy to take your prototype to your patent attorney to show how it works.

➤ A prototype will help you troubleshoot. My Hat Wrap backpack entertainer prototype was fashioned like a baby bib tied around a hat, with teethers and small stuffed shapes attached to the fabric. One of the shapes had a rattle inside it. When I tested out the prototype with the baby, the rattle was so close to my ear that it drove me crazy. I took it out.

➤ A prototype will help you refine and improve your idea. I heat-tested the adhesive tape I used for the car seat mirror in hot cars. I put it in my toaster oven too. Then I put it in the freezer to see if it would fail in extreme cold. This was valuable data, similar to the process big companies go through to test their products. Eventually, when I wanted to cut the cost, I ditched the adhesive and used a rivet instead. When you put together your sell sheet, you may be paying a graphic artist to do a drawing of your product, and it's a lot cheaper to change things at the prototype stage than it is to pay your artist to do version after version of it.

How to Make a Prototype

First, you might want to check out my YouTube videos that show how I developed my car seat mirror prototype. (Just go to my website—www. patricianolanbrown.com—and click the "YouTube" icon. Please "subscribe" to my channel for free.) You can start by making a cheap mock-up from cardboard and tape to get an idea of your product's shape and dimensions. You can also buy or find items around the house that are similar to what you're making to take apart and rebuild to make your prototype and then retrofitting, tweaking, and refining them until you get it right (for instance, my kids' toys were a great resource here). For my car seat mirror prototype, I experimented with locker mirrors, bike mirrors, and auto mirrors. When you're looking for materials for your prototype, you can do what I do and spend time in The Home Depot, or any hardware store—I can usually find anything I need there. When you're at the hardware store, don't be afraid to think outside the box: try the plumbing aisle to find lots of interesting plastic shapes, for instance. You can also check out Thomas-net.com—a great online resource for components.

One big breakthrough for product developers trying to make a prototype is the 3-D printer. The costs have come way down, so they'll soon be common in homes. They can be used to make all kinds of plastic parts (like appliance replacement parts, for instance).

I used coffee cup sleeves for my first prototype of the Parachute Dog, and I started out testing chip clips for the bottom clip that holds the used waste bag, but quickly realized that they needed to be stronger. Then I noticed that my badge holder at an event was a really strong compact clip. I general-searched, got samples, and voilà: they were just the right strength. These clips have a hole in them, so I made this the attachment point to the nylon pouch—and I found the perfect pouch while browsing in stores, where I discovered a camera bag that was just the right size to hold the unused bags. I bought a few, contacted the manufacturer, and bought a bunch very cheaply (you'll learn more about this in Chapter 14).

When it came time to make a prototype of the Hat Wrap baby entertainer, I had no clue how to sew—but I needed to be able to make a pattern and sew on straps and attachments. (In junior high, I took woodworking instead of sewing.) So I took a sewing class, bought a used sewing machine, and ta-da! I was able to make my prototype. That's when I learned that woodworking, sewing, and visual arts are just as important to an inventor as are math and science classes.

All of my ideas were easy to make, so I could make a "real" prototype that was very close to the finished product. If your idea is simple enough, you can do the same—and that means you can start contacting companies that sell the stuff you need to make your actual product, and get quotes and free samples. This will also give you a good idea of what your real materials will cost. When I began contacting suppliers, I asked for their suggestions and found out how helpful people could be; for instance, suppliers sent me several different options of adhesives to test. When I general-searched "plastic mirrors" to find samples that would work for my idea I was surprised at how generous the suppliers were, and how many different thicknesses of mirrors I was sent.

You can rent time and/or space in a machine/wood/metal shop complete with experienced people ready to help you if needed. Or you can become a member of an organization that rents space and tools. These often offer classes, too. The one in my neck of the woods is called Artisan's Asylum (www.artisansasylum.com), a nonprofit community craft studio, but you can do a little online research to see what's available in your area. Or you could give the project to a high school or vocational wood shop, or look into the shops available at retirement communities.

A Word of Warning

If you have young children, be careful not to leave anything dangerous lying around the house. I once made a prototype all-natural deodorant and put it in the fridge covered with plastic wrap. The next morning when I went to retrieve it, I noticed there were crumbs of it on the floor in front of the fridge. It turns out that one of my youngsters thought it was feta cheese and ate some! Fortunately, it was just coconut oil and baking soda, so there was no harm done.

Once you have a decent product prototype, you might want to prototype your packaging, too. This is a part of the process that I really enjoy. Before you begin, go back to the list you compiled during your store-research stage, which will tell you what kind of packaging is preferred at the store where you imagine your product selling. Just remember that if you go the licensing route, the licensee will be using its own packaging, so you may not want to invest too much time, effort, or money at this stage. However, if you plan to sell your product yourself, packaging will be crucial.

You can go to a printer and have that company make a mock-up package based on a dimensional drawing, or you can have the printer design a package from your prototype, which most are willing to do as long as you also use that company to do the printing. The fastest and easiest thing to do, though, is to find existing products that have an appropriate package for your prototype. Then you can just buy whatever the packaging is housing. For example, I found a perfect setup that had dog toys inside, so I bought half a dozen. Another time I noticed packages of jump ropes that would be a perfect size for one of my other ideas, so I bought a bunch of those as well. I gave away the dog toys and jump ropes as gifts and used the packaging for my prototype, with printouts designed by my graphic artist glued on. The final result looks great and very professional. You'll find out more about designing your graphics in the next section of this chapter.

WHAT TO DO WITH YOUR FINISHED PROTOTYPE

You will be using the prototype to demonstrate your product to your patent attorney and/or manufacturers—although you should never send out a prototype unsolicited or unprotected. Soon you'll find out how to use the prototype to pitch your idea, but for now, here are two great exercises to boost your confidence:

> ➤ Choose one store where you'd like to see your product sold. Take your prototype and put it on a shelf, then snap a photo of it sitting there. Put the photo in your Courage Bowl.

➤ Put your prototype where you'll see it last thing at night and first thing in the morning. I keep mine on a shelf in my bedroom. Seeing it with fresh eyes sometimes reveals a new benefit, feature, or tweak.

➤ I always keep my prototypes as keepsakes that remind me of how far a finished product has come.

➤ Now that you've done your research and made your prototype, you're ready to start the process of interfacing with licensees, buyers, and customers. The rest of this chapter explains just how to do that.

MAKE A SELL SHEET

Sell sheets are simple, short, and snazzy. These one-page tantalizers are meant to make people practically drool over your idea—and to *want* it. A sell sheet includes a pithy benefit statement, illustrations and/or photos, a demo video (for a digital version), a bulleted list of features, and your contact information—but not enough details that someone could rip off your idea.

The simplest version of the sell sheet is aimed at potential licensees. If you are going to use your sell sheet to seduce store buyers or tradeshow attendees, you will need to include a bit more information. See Chapter 13 for what to include in a beefed-up sell sheet.

Here are the basics for creating a compelling sell sheet:

Name your product. The name can be either descriptive or fun. What's most important is that it's not the same as anyone else's trademarked name, so you'll need to check to be sure it's all yours. If your product is picked up by a licensee, it may end up with an entirely different name, but that's fine; you still need a place to start.

Checking a Name to See if It's Trademarked

Before you do all of the following, it's wise to make sure the domain name for your website is available (see below). Then, if you want to do this research yourself, go to www.uspto.gov and click on Trademarks, then click on Trademark Search, then click on Basic Word Mark Search, and then type in the name you want to use. It will tell you if that name is alive or dead. If it's dead you can use it. If it's alive, and in the same class of goods as yours, you can't use it, so change your product name! For example, if I have a shampoo I want to call "Pizzazz" but there is already a breakfast cereal called "Pizzazz," that's okay—it's not the same class of goods. But if there is a hair gel called "Pizzazz," I can't use that name for my shampoo. However, it's always best to avoid using familiar or well-known names, even if the name you want to use is in a different class of goods, because big corporations might have the money to protect a product name across all classes. The safest possible route is to have a professional search done, usually through your attorney, and this will cost you in the neighborhood of $500. A professional search will cover you in ways that those outside the legal profession don't know about or have access to.

Since you will be setting up a website, you will get a free domain name, but you may want to keep that name pretty general. Also, because you may have other product ideas, you might want to choose a domain name for your overall website that's different from your product name (for instance, I own patricianolanbrown.com, and that's the umbrella for many products). But at this stage, when I've chosen a name for my product, I go ahead and buy a specific domain name for it for a year, or the shortest amount of time available, since domain names are cheap and once you own one no one else can use it. If the domain name is already taken, now's the time to change your product name. I usually also trademark the product name, and I've often been able to offer that name to a licensee. Trademarking your product name and grabbing a domain name might sweeten the pot for a licensee, and if you decide to sell the product yourself, it gives you the ability to build your own company around it (to find out how to trademark your product name, see Chapter 12). While you're at it, use this name for your Twitter account, Facebook page, and any other social media platforms that you might promote it on (see Chapter 16). Here's a fun product name story: you know the NERF foam products? Well, NERF actually stands for "Non-Expanding Recreational Foam." That's a mouthful for anybody. Can you imagine walking into a store and saying, "Excuse me, can you tell me where to find the Non-Expanding Recreational Foam bats, please?" Nope, didn't think so. "NERF" was a perfect solution.

Checking a Domain Name to See if It's Available

All domain sites are connected, so you can go to www.godaddy.com or www.networksolutions.com and type in the name you want to use in the space provided. If it's already taken, change your product name and try again! For more about domains, see Chapter 16.

Decide on a style for the sell sheet. The sell sheet must grab the reader's attention immediately, and the style of it should reflect your product. For example, if your idea is for a toy, the sheet could be colorful, with a cartoonlike illustration and lively typeface. For a new tool or kitchen device, it could be more straightforward. My original background was in graphic design, so I had an advantage here and could do this myself, but it will probably make more sense for you to hire someone whose business is design rather than spending your time struggling with it yourself. I suggest working with a graphic artist. Now is a good time to start cultivating a relationship with a graphic artist because as you and your business grow, you'll need logos, drawings, tradeshow signs, business cards, and more. Graphic artists are hired per project or hourly, and they should keep up with all the new computer programs, file requirements, and web design. Just make sure the designer you choose signs a provision that assigns all the rights to you, the inventor, to prevent confusion about who owns rights to your product or can claim co-inventorship. You can hire a graphic artist sight unseen over the Internet, but it's better to go with one who comes recommended by a person you trust. The designer is going to be an integral part of your team, and you need to choose someone you feel comfortable with, and whose portfolio you like.

If you absolutely can't afford a pro, you could go to your local college, vocational school, or high school and hire a newbie for next to nothing—and give a beginner a chance to build a portfolio. Or *you* can do it free: general-search "product sell sheets" and click on "images." There you'll find a whole slew of different designs. Choose one you love and try to emulate the layout yourself. Doing that will help you begin to develop your "look" or brand. A simple Microsoft Word program can be used for the layout.

Craft a benefit statement. Grab the list you made during your research that tells what your product is and what it does that sets it above the competitors. Now narrow down all these benefits into one strong, direct, enticing sentence. This is your benefit statement. Here are some examples from a few of my own products:

HAT WRAP—Wraps around any hat, protecting hair and jewelry, while entertaining baby in the backpack.

BACKPACK SAFETY MIRROR—Lets you quickly view your baby in a backpack.

PARACHUTE DOG— An earth-friendly, easier, neater dog waste cleanup kit.

Once you've written this statement, pat yourself on the back and put a copy of it into your Courage Bowl.

Include visuals. It's important to show an image of your product being used, so you can add a professional drawing by the graphic designer you've chosen, or use a Photoshopped image of what it would look like. If you've ended up with a great-looking prototype, you can photograph it, but this isn't mandatory: you're really just selling an idea. You can also take a photo of a less-than-perfect prototype and trace it to create your own illustration. For online versions of sell sheets, demo videos are becoming more and more popular, and you can make your own with a cheap video camera or phone—it doesn't have to be polished or expensively done. You just need to be sure that you at least have an NDA signed by the recipient before you send it out. Let me emphasize that this is an excellent way to go, since it's like making your own TV commercial showing the product in action. See my Parachute Dog demo videos, for example, at ParachuteDog.com. (See Chapter 16 for directions for making your own video.)

Add bullet points. If you want to add a few more advantages offered by your product, a bullet-point list is simple and eye-catching. Just keep it short and remember this has to explain your product and grab your reader in a few seconds. The trick is to make them want it without getting into too many fine details.

Include contact information. On the bottom of the sheet put all your contact information. If you don't want to include your home address, a P.O. box at your local post office is an inexpensive option. Now is the time to start thinking about a possible company name and logo, but your own name may do for now—Jane Doe Products, for example, leaves you plenty of wiggle room for future product ideas. And a personal cell phone number is fine: you just don't want your three-year-old answering a home phone. This is also where you will mention your trademarks, patents, or patents pending, if any. It's also where you'll place your website address and perhaps one or two of your main social media addresses.

So now you have a list of potential licensees, or you're ready to produce the product yourself. You have your prototype and your sell sheet. Before you start e-mailing or snail mailing potential licensees or buyers, the next step is crucial: protect it!

Protect It (Step Three)

Keep Thieves Away

The best lightning rod for your protection is your own spine.

—RALPH WALDO EMERSON

We live in a crazy culture that thrives on fear and tells us that everybody is a crook out to steal our ideas. When it comes to inventing, though, this kind of paranoia is actually healthy. By now, you have invested a lot of blood, sweat, and tears in your project, and you need to play it safe and protect it—and yourself. Trouble is, this is precisely the point in the process when people push the panic button and think they need a full (nonprovisional) patent *right away*. That isn't true. In fact, in some circumstances, getting a full patent may not be the best first step. I like to do preliminary research first and file for a provisional patent application (PPA; see the information on doing research in Chapter 11). Remember that a

patent doesn't guarantee that your idea is marketable, though, so your research is especially important. Sometimes people start throwing thousands of dollars at scoundrels who say they'll get a patent for them and then run off with their hard-earned money, laughing merrily all the way. Even if you do get a patent out of a deal with one of these middlemen, it may not be the best-quality patent, and the process will end up costing you way more than it should have. That's one of the reasons I wrote this book: to show you the simplest, least expensive way to keep your ideas safe. You don't even necessarily have to get a full patent (which is the most expensive option) in order to be adequately protected.

So here's what you need to know and do in order to keep your project floating along on a nice watertight boat, safe from the circling sharks. You can begin by going online to www.uspto.gov, the online go-to resource for inventors, and clicking on the Inventors tab at the top of the home page to check out the wealth of information under each category. Here is where you can find out about the different kinds of patents. This website looks complicated—and it is—but don't be intimidated! The site exists to help you, and it's good to know that this country encourages and supports individual inventors; you get the same playing field as the big corporations. In fact, it's cheaper for an independent inventor to apply for a patent than it is for a large corporation.

There is an overwhelming amount of information out there, so this chapter is designed to help you break things down into manageable bites. Here are some good basics about protecting your darling, starting with the simplest things and working up to the most complex.

NON-DISCLOSURE AGREEMENT (NDA)

What It Is: An NDA is (usually) a two-page legally binding mutual agreement designed to protect your ideas and trade secrets. It's essential to have signed NDAs in hand before you share your ideas with others, especially if you don't have a PPA or a full patent yet. But even if you do, it's still a good idea. You need two copies of the NDA for every company or person you contact. Both copies will be signed by both of you, and you each keep one copy. There is often a time limit of a few years on these; nobody should expect an NDA to be enforceable forever.

Why You Need One: If people you show your concept to try to pull a fast one and run away with your idea, they are punishable by law—*if* they signed an NDA. It also protects the company you're showing your product to; if that company is working on a similar product, the NDA protects them from inventors claiming the company stole their idea. So you can see how valuable this is for both parties!

How to Get One: Most companies you submit your idea to will have their own NDA for both of you to sign (and this is a good indicator that they're open to taking outside ideas). Make sure you read the NDA carefully. If you have any questions or see any red flags, contact the company for explanations.

If you need an NDA of your own, you can pay an attorney to draw one up for you (for a fee), or you could do what I did and general-search the forms available online and then download and print them out at no cost. Just be sure the form you choose includes the word "confidential." You'll need to fill in the name of each company or individual you're going to

show your product to, as well as the name of your state, since you will want the NDA to be governed by the laws in your home state.

Those who plan to pursue a license agreement for their idea may decide to stop right here: with an NDA in hand and a great sell sheet, you may feel you have enough to conquer the world. Certainly this is one strategy. But I've always believed there are a lot of good reasons to get your product name, logo, and/or phrase trademarked, and to file at least a PPA (more about that below), even if you just want to license. Why? Well, it gets you a first-to-file date. It gets you "patent pending" status. And it gives you a year to tweak and test your product. You're building a portfolio of intellectual property with the hope of making money on it, and if your materials are protected, you're bringing more to the table and sweetening the pot for potential licensees, which may nab you a better deal. In addition, you'll be taking steps toward building your own business, which you can also eventually sell to a licensee. So keep reading before you make your final decision.

TRADEMARK

What It Is: A trademark (™) tells the world that you own the name of your product, and it should ensure that nobody else can use that name on a similar product. A trademark can also be used to protect a logo or phrase you've come up with. For example, in addition to trademarking the name of my car seat mirror, I trademarked the phrase "It's like having eyes in the back of your head."

Why You Need One: A trademark prevents somebody else grabbing and using the name, logo, or phrase that you chose. If you've done your research (see Chapter 11) and you're reasonably sure that nobody else owns or has been using the name you want to use, you need to get that trademark ASAP.

Note: Because I'm a graphic designer and love designing logos, I made them for all of my products in the early days, and trademarked them, too. But I've learned that licensees have their own design staffs and logos, so now I just trademark the basic words—like "Parachute Dog" for my waste-bag cleanup kit.

How to Get One and How Much It Costs: You can hire an attorney, not only to do your search, but to file your trademark for you. However, this will cost money (see the next section, "Filing Through an Attorney"). Here's how to do it yourself, step by step:

➤ Because you will apply for your trademark through www.uspto.gov, your first step is to go online and check out this site.

➤ You should already have searched on the uspto.gov site, or paid for a professional search, to be sure your word, name, phrase, or logo is available (see Chapter 11). If you haven't done this, do it now!

➤ Under the Trademarks tab on the uspto.gov site, click on "trademark process." This will tell you step by step what you need to do. The highlighted links even include helpful videos that thoroughly explain all the terms on your application (like "Goods and/or Services" or "Filing Basis").

➤ While still on the uspto.gov site, find out what class of goods your creation will fall under by looking in the online manual. Or look up the trademarked names of similar products that you see in the store (for instance, if you've come up with a better toothbrush, look

up the names of other toothbrushes) and find out the class of goods they're registered under.

➤ When you're ready to file, go to the Trademarks tab, click "online filing," and then click on "initial application form."

➤ Go through the application carefully, making notes about what you'll need, and writing down any questions that come up. Be sure to call the toll-free number for the Inventors Assistance Center— 800-PTO-9199—with your questions, or if you need help filling out the forms.

➤ If you make a mistake, it's no big deal: you can delete the form any time before you pay and try again.

➤ When everything is filled out correctly and you're ready to file, get out your credit card and go for it.

Once you've completed your application, you will receive a confirmation and can begin using the trademark symbol (™) after your product name. Then the name will go through an examination process, and you may be asked to clarify something. Read any correspondence you receive carefully and contact the examiner if you need something explained. The final approval process can take up to four years, but at the end of it, your product name becomes a registered trademark (®). You'll get a very official-looking sealed document in the mail when this happens. Sweet!

As of this writing, the filing fee starts at $275 per class of goods, with other maintenance fees due between the fifth and sixth years and again between the ninth and tenth.

Filing Through an Attorney

Fees vary, but to give you a rough idea, I recently spoke to my patent attorney and he told me that the attorney search alone costs at least $500 and takes one to two weeks. On top of that, filing the form through this attorney would cost $1,450 per single class of goods and services! If you have additional classes, it would run you an additional fee per class with more fees due if you have extensions or need other forms filed. The time frame was another 30 days. So you would have been looking at about a month and a half and around $2,000 plus—which is why I did it myself.

Warning: You need to keep a close eye on the market to make sure nobody is using your protected property. Remember, this is not your attorney's job—it's yours! Even though you now own a trademark, you still have to be vigilant. A few years ago, I noticed that a baby clothing company was using my trademarked name. Since its products were in the same class as my Hat Wrap, I knew I had the right to say, "Hey, that's mine!" but I didn't want a big, costly legal battle, either. I asked my attorney what to do, and he told me to let the company know that I owned the name and wanted the company to stop using it. This is known as a "cease and desist" notification. I typed up a simple letter, sent it to the company, and lo and behold, it stopped using the name—and it only cost me a stamp! Let this be a cautionary tale: the baby clothing company probably didn't do the research that I recommended in Chapter 11, so then it had to change all its printed material, clothing labels, packaging—everything. All because the company didn't do its research.

HIRING A PATENT ATTORNEY

You can certainly get your product name, phrase, or logo trademarked, and your NDA downloaded, all by yourself. I did. But I highly recommend that at every step in the protection process after this point you call on the help and services of a vitally important member of your team: your patent attorney.

What It Is: Not every attorney is a patent attorney. The reason is that patent law is, frankly, pretty convoluted and it takes someone who is an expert in it to wade through it all. So be sure when you start your search for legal assistance that you're looking not just for any old attorney, but for one whose specialty is patent law and who is registered to practice it. Not only that, patent attorneys have to pass a specialized bar exam, and hold degrees in engineering, physical science, or the equivalent in addition to their law degree, so they'll understand how things work.

What's a Patent Agent, and How Is That Different from a Patent Attorney?

A patent agent is not an attorney, but often is just as well qualified to conduct searches and write patents. The catch is that patent agents can't do anything that could be construed as "practicing law" (because they're not attorneys), which means they can't conduct patent litigation in court or draw up licensing contracts.

For my money, I'd rather hire a patent attorney, because she or he has a bigger bag of tricks and a wider scope of activity.

Why You Need One: Legalese, especially the legalese employed in the service of patent law, is a very complex and arcane language. Unless you speak it fluently, you run the risk of making costly mistakes. When you think about it, there's a reason lawyers make things so difficult for the layperson to understand: it's so we'll have to hire them. But, cynicism aside, a good patent attorney is knowledgeable about how things work and knows the best way to cover your invention. She or he will be your best ally from here on out, well qualified to give you the best advice, to be helpful and supportive, and to be in your corner should any legal trouble arise.

How to Find One: Back when people were still using phone books, that's how I found my attorneys: in my local yellow pages. Now you can do a search online, or rely on the best kind of advertising—word of mouth. If someone you trust knows a great patent lawyer, start there. If you do an online search, you can also scour the Web for articles written by or about your possible attorneys and see what they have to say for themselves, or what others have to say about them.

Criteria for Choosing the Right One: The most important consideration, besides general competence and knowledge in your area of invention, is feeling that you and your attorney have a good rapport. You need to trust that she or he listens to you and genuinely respects and cares about what you have to say, even while occasionally disagreeing with you in order to steer you in the right direction. Certainly ask for references, but trust your instincts: if you don't get along with your attorney, it won't matter how expert that person is.

Money Concerns: It helps if your attorney will accept payment in increments rather than expecting a lump sum up front. Also, it's preferable to find an attorney who doesn't have huge overhead (translation: an enormous office

with a view of the best scenery in town), so you won't be charged for every phone call (unless you're the kind of inventor who calls two or three times a day). While you're interviewing patent attorneys, be sure to ask if the initial consultation will be free. Many do this, and depending on your attorney's hourly rate, it can add up to substantial savings.

Time Concerns: It's ideal for an attorney to answer your questions in a day or two rather than allowing your e-mails to languish in the inbox for weeks. Time is of the essence.

Once you've narrowed down your list of possible attorneys, go back to your old friend uspto.gov and check to make sure your choices are registered to practice: https://oedci.uspto.gov/OEDCI. Attorneys listed in this section of the site have all the necessary legal, scientific, and technical qualifications, and are in good standing. In other words, uspto.gov has done some preliminary quality control for you.

DIFFERENT TYPES OF PATENTS

Most of you will only be dealing with the first kind in the following list, but it's good to know that there are actually three different types of patents issued by the USPTO. Each is meant to protect a different type of invention.

1. Utility—New and useful process, machine, article of manufacture, or composition of matter, or any new and useful improvements.

2. Design—New, original, and ornamental design for an article of manufacture.

3. Plant—Asexually reproduced distinct and new variety of plant.

For more comprehensive definitions and information, visit www.uspto.gov.

The "First Inventor to File" Law and What It Means for You

Once upon a time, inventors had to prove they were the first to come up with an idea, which meant convoluted record-keeping and rigorous paper trails. Well, the emphasis (and the law) has changed. Now whoever files first gets the prize. In other words, even if you can prove you have the idea for a wonderful widget, a competitor who files for a patent before you do gets the rights. That is why you need to file a provisional patent application as soon as you feel comfortable doing so, often right after you've done the research to prove that your product or idea is not already out there, and that it's marketable. (Some people choose to get the PPA before they've even done the research. It's more of a risk, but it guarantees that they'll get an early filing date.)

PROVISIONAL PATENT APPLICATION (PPA)

What It Is: The PPA gives you a filing date and a "patent pending" status, which you can print on all your materials, including your sell sheet. Compared to the full patent (the correct term is "nonprovisional patent") process, it is a fairly inexpensive and fast way to get protection for your product. However, it doesn't turn into an issued patent automatically; you need to file for the nonprovisional patent within one year. There's really no such thing as a provisional patent—just an application.

A Word of Warning

All of the information in this chapter applies to United States trademarks and patents only. I've never worried about foreign patents because I was told by my attorney that it costs a fortune—and I make sure my license agreements cover royalties for all countries. The United States is a huge enough market anyway. But if you're in doubt about foreign laws, ask your patent attorney for advice.

Why You Need One: When I first started out, the PPA didn't even exist, so it wasn't an option. Now I'm a big fan of getting a PPA. There are several compelling reasons why. The new first-inventor-to-file law means that you need to get your application to the officials first: if you get all tied up with the lengthy full-patent process, somebody else could get in there before you. Also, most investors and licensees prefer to deal with products that are protected. In fact, many licensees and product submissions companies will *only* consider protected ideas, so it gives you more clout at the same time that it fends off the competition. In other words, it gives you a lot of the benefits of a full patent without the big cost, and it's more flexible.

Once you file for a PPA, you technically have one year to file for a full or nonprovisional patent, and the clock starts ticking as soon as you file. Keep in mind, though, that it can take your attorney as long as five months to prepare for filing a full or nonprovisional patent, so you really have more like seven months. This means it's super-important for you to have done your research prior to filing. But during this seven-month window, you can test your idea, tweak and revise it, and try to find a licensee. If your product ends up changing significantly, you can even file for a new PPA and use the combination when you file for the full or nonprovisional patent. Once you file that nonprovisional patent, though, you can't change your product in any way without paying extra fees and jumping through more hoops to amend it.

How to Get One and How Much It Costs: While you can go to uspto.gov and file for a PPA all by yourself for a low, low filing fee of a little more than $100, I strongly recommend you cover yourself by working with your patent attorney, because any missteps through inexperience could end up costing you a whole lot more than what you would have paid a reputable patent attorney. A PPA must have a good written description of the invention, plus drawings, and it has to support the NPA (full patent). The ballpark figure for an attorney-handled PPA is roughly $2,000. This isn't cheap, but it's worth it. My attorney will apply some PPA fees to a nonprovisional patent if applicable, so be sure to ask yours if that is a possibility.

Note: Many patent attorneys may urge you to go straight for a full/nonprovisional patent. They may recommend that partly because they'll make more money that way, but also because if that's your final goal, and if you're sure your product will not change (or you have the money and time to cover amending the patent), it could save you some time and money in the long run. However, if you intend to find a licensee that will take on the product under a PPA, or if you want to test the market first, and if you want to secure the earliest filing date, stand firm on just wanting the PPA for now.

FULL/NONPROVISIONAL PATENT

What It Is: This is the highest level of protection available for your product. The legalese for what it does is "excludes others from making, using, offering for sale, selling, or importing" your invention. In other words, it announces "hands off!" to anybody who wants to swipe your idea.

Most of you will apply for a utility patent, which is granted to "anyone who invents or discovers any new and useful process, machine, article of manufacture, composition of matter or any new and useful improvement thereof."

Why You Need One: If you want to license your product, you *don't* necessarily need a nonprovisional patent right away! Hopefully you can negotiate with your licensee about the fees for getting a full patent, although you'll want to make sure that you will still be using your own attorney for the process, and that you'll own it and it will be in your name. But if you want to build your own business around your product and manufacture and distribute it yourself, you will eventually want the legal protection of a full/nonprovisional patent. Just remember that a patent has nothing whatsoever to do with the marketability of an idea, so if your research shows that your product isn't going to sell well, a patent is an unnecessary expense.

How to Get One and How Much It Costs: Don't even think about trying to do this yourself. You need a good patent attorney, and you will end up paying a substantial amount. The fee is likely to go up depending on the complexity of your product.

The Full/Nonprovisional Patenting Process

Getting a full-on patent doesn't happen overnight, even with a patent attorney at the helm. First your attorney will want to do an exhaustive patent search, for two reasons: First, to be sure your product doesn't infringe on anyone else's patent; second, to make sure your idea is patentable—sufficiently new and different—on its own. You'll need to give your attorney your sketches and sell sheet (and a prototype or a video showing how your product works), along with a check for the search fee, which will vary from attorney to attorney. The search usually takes three to six weeks, after which the attorney will meet with you to give you a review of the search results as well as what she or he thinks your odds are of getting a patent on your idea and whether or not you're infringing on anyone else's. Searches often will turn up products so close to your own that your attorney may advise you to stop right there. I've had this happen to me and, as you may remember from Chapter 8, I persisted anyway and got the patent. But in some cases, it really is best to cut your losses and start over with a new idea. Trust your instincts: if an existing patent is too similar to yours, don't beat your head against the wall. Use your energy to develop a new idea. Sadly, though, the fee you paid for the attorney to do the search is nonrefundable.

After the thorough search, if you decide to move forward with the process, you and your attorney will prepare and file the application package. This step can take one to three months, and fees depend on the complexity of your product. The low end is somewhere in the range of $5,000. Your attorney will usually expect half of the payment when you start the process.

Once the patent has been filed, you can use the words "Patent Pending" on your materials—a good deterrent against others trying to filch your idea. Now the Patent Office gets involved. For approximately two to five years, the Office "dialogues" with your attorney to evaluate the patentability of your idea. Be forewarned: the word on the street is that the preliminary evaluation by the Patent Office is usually negative. The Office usually wants changes, citing several preexisting patents. Your attorney will have already examined these, though, and will prepare a (hopefully successful) rebuttal, with your help and input. This rebuttal will include amendments and a technical brief explaining why your invention is different from the patents dredged up by the Patent Office, and it may cost you anywhere from a thousand dollars or less to a boatload.

If you and your attorney get approval, you'll get a Notice of Allowance in the mail, after which you have three months to submit an issue fee (around $885), a draftsperson's fee for the person preparing the formal drawings (around $700), and a publication fee (around $300). Several months after this, the Patent Office will issue your patent.

Remember that it is your responsibility to explain your product to the best of your ability to the attorney. After all, it's a new product, so your attorney can't possibly be expected to know how it works. You will need to read every single word your attorney writes about your product and examine every drawing from the hired draftsperson to be sure everything is accurate.

At the end of your PPA year, if you haven't found a licensee, you need to be prepared to pay for the nonprovisional patent route yourself, or to drop the whole thing. Even if you do have a licensee who will pick up the fees for your patent, you want to make sure that you and your attorney will still be generating the application for it. And keep in mind that everybody's fees tend to rise with time.

TWO FINAL WORDS ON PLAYING IT SAFE

First, whether you license your product or make it yourself, it's a smart idea to stash away some of your profits just in case legal difficulties arise. The truth is that anything can be argued in court and you may need to defend your property further down the line, so having a chunk of change handy means you can hire the best patent litigator available if you need to.

Second, be forewarned that as soon as you get a trademark or a patent, your name somehow gets placed on lists kept by crafty shysters who will flood your mailbox with official-looking mail—and most of it will be telling you about fees you supposedly have to pay. This is a hoax! Report it to uspto.gov. Never send money through the mail: you can pay the legitimate fees you really do owe directly to uspto.gov online or through your patent attorney.

Pitch It (Step Four)

Make 'Em Want It Bad

Do you want to know who you are? Don't ask. Act! Action will delineate and define you.

—THOMAS JEFFERSON

"Pitching" is the insider term for presenting your product idea to people who could conceivably buy it. And it's tremendously important. Why? Because no matter how marvelous your product idea is, if nobody knows it exists, it won't go anywhere. It always grieves me to think of all the great little gizmos lying around gathering dust because their inventor didn't pitch them properly—and so the public isn't aware they exist. One thing for sure: your brainchild deserves better than this! Languishing in obscurity is not how you want the story of your product to end.

Whether you're looking for a licensee to take it on, or you've decided to sell it to stores and/or customers yourself, pitching is crucial. This chapter will show you how to give a strong and convincing pitch that

will make people sit up and say, "Wow, what a great idea! This will sell! And I want it!"

You can go two ways here, and both require making cold calls and doing pitches:

Some inventors just want to be idea people, and don't even bother with filing PPAs—they just do cold calls and pitches until they get enough interest from a licensee that they get a signed non-disclosure agreement (NDA) from that company. Then they send out a sell sheet and hope to get licensed—and if they do, they let the licensee worry about protecting the idea. If that doesn't happen, they cut their minimal losses and go on to the next idea. And that's fine. If you're in this group, you only need to read the sections in this chapter titled "Cold Calls" and "The Pitch."

If you have filed for a provisional patent application (PPA), you can shout about your product from every rooftop (although you still need to know the basics of cold calling and pitching). If you're in this second group, it's not as crucial for you to get a signed NDA first because you're already protected and can begin promoting your product in press releases; in advertising, including free advertising (you'll learn about these methods later in this chapter); on your website (more about social media in Chapter 16); during radio and television appearances; at trade shows; all over the Internet; and more.

Whichever route you decide to take, this chapter will give you some tools and tips to ace your pitch everywhere you give it.

COLD CALLS

Even the name makes people shiver! Brrr! The thought of picking up the phone and reaching out to a total stranger and trying to convince her or him that your product is all that and a bag of chips makes many of us so nervous we have to beat a path for the bathroom. Relax. I'll tell you how to warm up those cold calls and connect with the human beings on the other end of the line.

First, the cold call basics.

Why do them at all? The goal is to get to a decision maker (someone in charge of new product submissions) so you can pitch your product then and there, or schedule a phone interview to pitch it and get that person so interested that she or he will sign an NDA (especially if you don't have a PPA), want more information, and eventually buy it. Cold calls may start out cold, but they establish friendly contact with other human beings and they start building your relationship with the company you're interested in. They also guarantee both real attention for your product and safety: if you send unsolicited information, your precious idea is likely to end up discarded or, worse, stolen. No—you want companies or buyers to want your product and ask for information. Your first entry point is the phone.

Why not just send an e-mail? Everybody does stuff online now, so why not? Well, there's one big reason: the personal touch is golden. What do *you* do when you get an unsolicited e-mail? That's right: you delete it unread. Or it ends up in your spam folder. Do your research and find out a little bit about their products and the name of the person you want to reach, and talk to them human-to-human. It beats the impersonality of an e-mail hands down. You can pretend you know the person you're talking to, be yourself, and respond to the other person's questions and comments.

If you're pitching to potential licensees, it is becoming more common for companies to have a "submit new product idea" feature on their web-sites, usually under the Contact heading. Prior to submitting any info, they tell you to download their NDA and sign it first. But I prefer to have a per-

son-to-person phone conversation rather than sending anything beforehand. Once I've spoken to someone, I'll check out the company's NDA, sign it, and send information (although I prefer having a PPA filed prior to uploading anything online).

Are cold calls just for finding a licensee? No. Keep in mind that, although licensing your product might be your first choice or goal, the process often takes weeks or even months. You have to be persistent and make calls over and over. The problem with this is that once you file your PPA (if you do it at all), the clock is ticking on your patent deadline, so you only have a finite amount of time. Even after you get a signed NDA, some companies take up to 90 days, or even more, to decide whether or not to license. That's why I always suggest that you keep moving forward and approach many companies. Frankly, patience is not my strong suit, and I sometimes decided it was better to be proactive and build my own company around a product rather than waiting and waiting for someone to take it on. But even if you decide to start your own business, you'll still need to know how to do a cold call, because you'll want to interest buyers in your product. Cold calls are multipurpose!

Who do I call? Remember the list of manufacturers (the potential licensee list) you compiled when you did your research in Chapter 11? You're going to call each and every one of them. Also, Chapter 16 will tell you about the online phenomenon LinkedIn—a free social network for professional contacts, a sort of online directory, which is another great resource for possible licensees or store buyers for specific groups of products. Keep mail-order catalogs in mind as other possible purveyors of your product. They can be great segues to getting your product into stores, since store buyers give them a lot of credibility.

When you do start making those calls, keep a record of the date you called, the name of the person your spoke with, and what was said. You will spend a lot of time on this step, and you need to stay organized and create paper trails so you don't lose your way, and also just in case you need to prove something later on. Stay positive.

Gearing Up to Make a Cold Call

Be persistent. Chances are you won't have a chance to pitch your idea right off the bat. Most buyers and licensees are very busy people, and they're guarded by gatekeeper dragons whose job may be to turn you away. Just be super-polite and friendly and get to know their name, too. This is where persistence comes in: you'll be making a lot of follow-up calls. Once you've managed to talk to somebody who might conceivably be interested in your product, then you can do your pitch, but that can take a while. Work on maintaining a hopeful neutrality that minimizes disappointment.

Prepare your script. First, decide what you want to say.

To licensees: Ask to speak to the person in charge of new product submissions, or a product manager. Tell that person you're a product developer and you have something that would be a good extension of the licensee's existing line, or a good fit for the company. Or that your research shows that the company doesn't have a product like yours but its competitors do and yours is easier, better, quicker, cheaper, cooler, sexier, more updated, more clever—whatever is relevant and true.

To store buyers: Ask for the specific buyer's name that you've gleaned from your online research or from LinkedIn. Or contact the store owner or manager, if it's a smaller store. Tell the person you talk to

that you have developed a _____ that _____ (list benefits) and would be a great addition to the company's stores or a great item for a smaller store's customers.

Role play. To get over the stiffness and stage fright of talking to strangers, do what great performers do: rehearse. Find a friend and practice your script with that person until you start to feel relaxed. Many people dread this part, but practice makes perfect and my experience is that a pitch is your pal—and it's a place where your I.N.V.E.N.T. traits can shine, especially your voice. When you're actually on the phone with someone, just pretend you're still sitting in your living room talking to your friend. You'll do fine—and besides, if it starts going horribly wrong, you can hang up and then call back, saying the call dropped! Believe it or not, eventually this process will become fun and challenging because you have to think on your feet and it's stimulating—and as you practice saying your lines over and over they will start to flow out of you like magic.

Keep a positive mindset. Always remember that your product could make a lot of money for someone, and/or offer tangible benefits to an end user. What a great opportunity for the person on the other end of the line! You're giving her or him a chance that could be really useful.

Detach. Give yourself a realistic target goal—say, six cold calls a week (a completely arbitrary number; do more or fewer depending on how busy you are)—and then do that. Make it a part of your schedule: on Mondays do three calls, and another three on Wednesdays, or whatever works for you. As long as it's in your schedule, it's like exercising: you'll do it. Try to detach from the outcome. No matter what response you get, just keep to your target and keep making those calls. That way you'll have a feeling of accomplishment regardless of what happens.

Know what to expect. When you ask to speak to the person in charge of new product submissions, or to a product manager (or even someone in marketing or sales) for a licensee, or to a store buyer, here is what may happen next:

➤ *You get sent to voice mail. What to do:*

> The first time, hang up and try again later. The second time, same thing. The third time, leave a voice message of your script. Keep it very brief, but be sure to leave your contact information. Try again in a couple of days, leaving just one more voice message before you send an e-mail. Or try another contact name in the company.

➤ *You get a gatekeeper who won't connect you (for various reasons). What to do:*

> Ask for the name of the gatekeeper you're talking to, write it down, and say, "Thank you, _____ . Is there a better time to reach _____ ?" Write down that time and call back then. Also, get the e-mail address of the person you're trying to reach!

> Sometimes the people you're trying to reach aren't getting your messages, so send an e-mail to them directly, or try someone else in the pipeline. Never include detailed information; just give them the script. A hint: you will usually have better luck getting past a gatekeeper if you have the specific name or extension of someone to whom you want to speak. Adopt a masterful tone.

➤ *The gatekeeper does connect you. What to do:*

> Be prepared. If you know what the negative responses are likely to be, you can deal with them in a more positive way. Whatever happens, anyone you speak to deserves the courtesy of a friendly follow-up e-mail, thanking them for their time.

Here are the five most likely negative scenarios you'll get from licensees, followed by the best way to deal with them:

1. *We don't take outside ideas*. Ask if she or he knows anyone who might be interested. Then send a friendly thank-you e-mail, cut your losses, and move on.

2. *We only consider protected ideas*. You will probably hear this a lot, which is why I've recommended that you file for a PPA. Then you can truthfully say your idea is patent pending.

3. *Send us your patent application so we can see what you're doing*. Never send what you're claiming in a patent application while it's pending, because that gives it away. Tell them you've been advised against it, but that after you have a signed NDA you'd be happy to send more information.

4. *We'll keep your information on file for later consideration*. This is often a polite brush-off, but you can ask when the next product review might be and call back then. You can also follow this up with an e-mail that includes your sell sheet (as long as you have a PPA).

5. *We don't sign NDAs, so just send us all your detailed information*. This may be a red flag. Technically, if you have filed for a PPA you're protected, but if you haven't, then never, never, never send detailed information to anyone unless she or he has signed an NDA. I'm not necessarily saying that a company asking for information without an NDA is out to steal your idea, but never take the chance! Offer to provide an NDA if the company doesn't have one. Even if you have filed

for a PPA, I always recommend getting the extra protection of an NDA, although at that point it's not as crucial.

Here are likely negative responses from store buyers:

We don't have any room for new products right now. Ask when the buyer might start planning for the next buying cycle and make a note to call back then. Also, send a follow-up e-mail directing the buyer to your website or digital sell sheet (after seeing what you have to offer, the buyer may be impressed enough to make room for it!).

We already carry a product like that. Explain why yours is different and better and point the buyer to your demo video or offer to come in for a live demonstration (if the company is local).

And what do you do if you get a positive response (besides the fandango)?

If a licensee is interested, tell your contact person that once the NDA is signed by both of you, you would be happy to forward a sell sheet along with the URL for your demo video or website, or to pitch your product in person to tell the company all about it, and so on. This is the time to wow a potential licensee with any sales history, testimonials, or poll results on your product (I'll tell you how to do an online poll in Chapter 16), while reiterating that you're familiar with the company's products and would love to be part of its line.

If a store buyer is interested, try to get her or him to agree to at least a minimum order—more is of course better—and go over all the details of pricing, shipping, and payment terms that you have on your beefed-up sell sheet. Then go make the products!

THE PITCH

Whether you're trying to hook a licensee or a store buyer for your product, your greatest ally is the pitch, and you'll be delivering it in any number of venues and ways. But before you give 'em all you've got, you have to be sure everything is in place.

Once you have received an NDA from the company involved, read it carefully. If anything seems "off" or you need explanation, call the company or run it by your attorney. When you've figured it out and signed it, call again or e-mail to tell the company you've sent back the NDA and to set up an appointment to deliver your pitch on the phone or in person (although in-person pitches are getting to be rare). Be sure to thank your contact at the company.

When both you and the company have a copy of the signed NDA in hand, send in your sell sheet and the URL for your website (see Chapter 16) with a brief cover letter saying you're looking forward to telling the company more about your product on the day and time you've set up.

Now it's time to perfect your pitch. This is the performance you've been working toward, like an actor who has prepared for weeks and months to finally get up in front of an audience.

Here are the nuts and bolts of the pitch:

■ Remember the elevator pitch you wrote in Chapter 5? It's a great framework, so revisit it and add to it. Remember that the listeners want to know two things, and they need to get the answers immediately: What is it/what does it do/what makes it so great? And, even more important, how can I make money from it? The people listening to your pitch probably have your sell sheet in front of them, and if you have a demo video they can plug into, great. Also, people tend to believe in facts, so bring on the research you've done that shows why your product will be a big hit with consumers, and how it will make a tidy profit. This is the time to tell them all about it. For instance, when organic food first caught on in popularity, many enterprising organic snack product inventors were able to quote facts and figures that proved the trend of eating more healthy, organic food was on the rise. This is also the place for any testimonials, poll results, store buyer feedback, and any media coverage you've received. If you've done your prep work to figure out the likely cost of making your product and what you could reasonably charge for retail and wholesale, tell them all about it.

■ Practice with a friend so you feel comfortable, just as you did with the cold call. Remember that pitching is better than cold calls because the people you're going to eventually present it to already know a little bit about you, and they actually want to hear what you have to say!

■ Be sincere and enthusiastic. If you're nervous, tell your listeners that, but also be sure to let your genuine excitement for your idea shine. Basically, the pitch is a live sell sheet or commercial for your product, with lots of oomph and personality. You're the best person to do it, too, because you know your product intimately and you're passionate about its merits. It's also important to remember that you need to listen as well as pitch, avoid pushiness, and cultivate being able to respond to questions and feedback. If you're pleasant and sincere, people will often want to help you. Even if their company isn't a good fit, they may have recommendations for you.

■ Smile. Even if they can't see you, they'll feel the warmth in your voice.

■ Stay positive and keep pitching to other companies. To illustrate this point, I thought car seat manufacturers would be the ones to want my mirror, so they were first on my pitch-to list. One in particular really loved it

and spent months and months reviewing it, only to decide in the end not to pursue it. Of course I was disappointed, and the company wouldn't elaborate on the reason, either. My guess is that the company didn't want to admit that its product was flawed and needed the addition of my product! In any case, it was a good thing I was pitching it to other companies with baby travel and safety products, or I would have wasted a lot of valuable time.

The In-Person Pitch

Be imaginative. Although most pitches will be over the phone, you will probably have opportunities to do live demos and pitches as well. As you keep reading this chapter, you'll see how trade shows, conventions, and media appearances all offer those opportunities. And if you're selling the product yourself, you'll often contact local buyers face-to-face.

The biz is full of great stories of imaginative and memorable pitches. Take Sara Blakely, the inventor of Spanx, the popular women's slimming shapewear, for instance. After a lot of rejection from buyers, she decided to try a totally different approach—she took one of the female buyers into the ladies room, where she stripped down to her Spanx in order to demonstrate its benefits. Talk about impact! Needless to say, she got the order. And, depending on the crowd, when I demonstrate my Parachute Dog wastebag kit I sometimes use chunks of chocolate—which sweetens the performance all around and adds a little humor. It gets a great reaction every time, and makes the audience remember me and my product!

It can be worth it to give your pitch to the buyers at small specialty stores (to reach the buyers for a big-box store, you'll need to find them on LinkedIn or something similar). At one point, my husband and I went all up and down Cape Cod stopping at small baby stores along the way to show them the car seat mirror, and we sold a lot of them. Bring testimonials and samples and try to make the sale. If the owner or manager doesn't want to order your product yet, offer to give them a few and tell them you will only take your cut of the selling price if the products sell. This gives them an incentive to sell them (something you wouldn't be able to do in a big box store!). It will be a true test of possible interest in your product, and its potential sales capability.

You don't need to get torqued over your "performance." If your product is something a buyer likes, it will sell itself, as long as the buyer sees a potential for profit.

I have an inventor friend who calls stores or actually goes into them, pretending to be an ordinary customer and asking if the store carries his product. If the person at the store says no, he says it's a great product, the store should carry it, and he'll take his business to the store that has it! Which reminds me of the Toothpick Story: one of the early inventors of the toothpick used to call restaurants and ask to make a reservation. Then he would ask if the restaurant had toothpicks. If the person at the restaurant said no, he would cancel the reservation, saying he'd go somewhere that had them! (You wouldn't believe how many patents there are on toothpicks, but the first one in the pool had to create a demand for them.) Now more places have them than not. And don't even get me started on all the patents there are for toothpick holders.

One nice plus to interacting in person with someone is handing them your business card, and it's a good idea to have one to give them. I recommend MOO.com for unique, imaginative, nicely done cards, but of course there are other services you can use. Remember that a card is sometimes the first representation of your "brand" that people see, so you'll want to be sure yours is eye-catching enough to stand out. And, like your sell sheet, the card needs to include your logo and it needs to list your web address, your primary social networks, a phone number, and your email address.

Special Tips for Dealing with Store Buyers

■ If it's a local store you're contacting, offer to come in and give a personal demonstration.

■ You will be using your beefed-up version of the sell sheet here, including wholesale pricing, manufacturer's suggested retail price, shipping information, minimum order, the time it will take to get from order to delivery (lead time), how to order, and payment information. (It's good to specify a minimum order, since you don't want people buying just one at a time. I usually make my minimum for small stores a dozen.)

■ Smaller specialty stores are actually a great way to go. Big-box stores can be difficult to deal with; they usually won't take single items, since they want lines of products, and you need huge volume to make any profit. I found this out the hard way. One of my products was selling beautifully in small specialty stores, but then it got picked up by a big one. I was thrilled— but the small stores weren't, because suddenly my item was selling for less in the big store and it wasn't a high-end "specialty" product anymore. And then the big store ended up dropping it because I didn't have the inventory to support the volume it needed!

■ If the buyer is interested but on the fence about making a commitment, offer a discount on the first order, or free shipping.

■ If you've been selling directly to customers on your website but you'd like to get your product in stores, ask the customers who repeatedly order if they'd like to save shipping costs by going to their local store instead. Then ask them to suggest to the store that it carry your product. Voilà—instant sales force! And the stores will start calling you to order. I've had this happen a few times, since people would rather not pay for shipping every time they order. Even though you'll sell wholesale to stores, which means you won't make as much per item, you can make it up by requiring a minimum order.

PRESS RELEASES

Most people don't realize that the media are always scrambling to find new material. That's where you and your product idea can come in handy for them—and for you, too! Publicity is a lovely thing. It gives you credibility and builds recognition of your product while generating excitement for it. However, publicity doesn't usually come knocking at your door; you have to be proactive in going out there and getting some. A very effective way to do that is by writing a press release.

I discovered the wonderful world of writing press releases when my husband was driving home from work one night and heard an author on the radio talking about his book—which was about writing your own press releases. Tom suggested I get the book, which I did. In very short order I wrote my first press release, including two photos of my car seat mirror in use, with captions. I paid a little money for a company to distribute them, and paid for an envelope with "Warning: Airbags and Babies Don't Mix— Solution Inside" printed on it. Of course, this was back in the day before e-mailing was widespread. Now the press releases would go out over the Internet—and the line printed on the envelope would be the subject line.

That press release resulted in hundreds of articles being written about my product in major and minor newspapers and in parenting magazines. It was on newscasts and radio. Even Click and Clack, the Tappet Brothers, from the NPR radio show *Car Talk*, gave my car seat mirror a positive review. All of this coverage resulted in lots and lots of orders. Everything builds on itself, and the power of this kind of snowball effect can be really something!

What's a Press Release?

A press release is an article about your product, written in the third person and starting with a catchy heading, that promotes the product as something interesting, exciting, and newsworthy. Once you've written a press release, which should fit into a specific format that you can find online, you e-mail it to all the media contacts you can find in hopes that one will pick it up and publish it. You also can hire a company to distribute the press releases for you. Doing that can be extremely useful, but it can be prohibitively expensive, at least initially. Of course, before you hire anyone to do publicity or PR, you should do your due diligence by researching the company or individual and their credentials.

Researching the prospective firm can not only help you avoid the possibility of getting ripped off, it can also ensure that you're dealing with a professional who specializes in promoting your product to the right people.

Here's why it worked. A new product is automatically newsworthy to some degree, but if you can tie your product to a current event that's on people's mind you'll hit real pay dirt. When I first invented the car seat mirror, airbags weren't mandatory—so parents had the option of placing their infants beside them in the front seat. Then airbags did become mandatory and some terrible injuries and even fatalities resulted from those powerful airbags smashing into the passenger side car seats. The airbag/car seat problem was a big one, so I got a lot of attention right away for a product that would enable parents to keep their eye on their infant even if the child was in the back seat.

Another example involves my pet waste cleanup kit. I was able to generate press releases that linked the product to two current events: the banning of plastic bags by many communities (so people couldn't use them for carrying their dog's waste anymore), and the institution of fines for not picking up your dog's waste. My product solved two problems that were of concern to thousands of viewers and readers. And the media knew it.

To get started writing your own press release, revisit your sell sheet with fresh eyes. On a separate sheet of paper, list of all the benefits of your product that make it valuable. Now see if there's a "hook" that makes it newsworthy. What current problem does your product solve? Is there a human-interest angle? Does it tie in to a holiday or special event? Look at some examples of press releases online, or scan the article titles of magazines to get ideas. A compelling title is essential: you've got to be sure it grabs interest right away.

Once you've got a compelling subject line, write a short, content-rich rough draft. Be sure to include clickable links to your website, as well as "share" buttons for social media (see Chapter 16). Run it by a trusted cheerleader and keep working on it until it feels right. You have to stand out from the herd and make yourself and your product sound absolutely valuable and fascinating.

Once you've written your release, you can go two routes:

1. Send it yourself to local newspapers, radio stations, television stations, and reputable and popular blogs and websites (related to your product or your product's interest group). It should be easy to find out the names and e-mail addresses of contact people.

2. Use a company like PRWeb.com to distribute it farther afield; otherwise you'll be spending hours researching possible media contacts. The same company can also write your release for you, but it will cost you more money—and I believe you're the best person to generate excitement for your product because you know it better than anyone and believe in it with all your heart and soul.

3. Remember that you can also write press releases about events you're attending. These will be especially valuable for your local media ("Local Inventor Shows Her New Gizmo at Dallas Trade Show" will probably get some interest in your hometown). As you continue to grow your brand, send a press release to the media any time you get a product or personal award or nab a business deal.

4. Be sure to send any press releases you write to all your social media contacts, too. I'll tell you more about that in Chapter 16.

5. Good press releases can lead to articles and orders, as well as online, radio, and television appearances. They're the magic beans that can grow quite a beanstalk!

TRADE SHOWS

I love trade shows! I don't go every year—mostly only when I have a new product to launch—but over the years, I've learned my way around them, figured out how to work them to get lots of great attention for my products, and discovered how to enjoy the heck out of them. Now I can tell you everything you need to know in order to use trade shows effectively. They're a great way to get your product in front of the perfect target audience, and have a great time into the bargain.

What's a Trade Show?

Sometimes they're called an expo or a trade exhibition, but they're basically an indoor fair. The big international shows run over the course of several days, with dozens or even thousands of tables and booths filled with vendors trying to gain the attention of the licensees, manufacturers, store buyers, and consumers who haunt these things looking for the next great idea, all under one roof. Although there are smaller trade shows here and there, I recommend saving your money for a big one.

There are trade shows for many, many kinds of products—practically every industry under the sun has at least one or two major shows per year—and it all adds up to around 10,000 of them happening around the country. They generate lots of media attention (the car shows in Detroit, for instance, consistently grab spots on national television news) and they are swarming with people who conceivably could want your product. There's just no excuse not to give it a try, armed with the tips and hints I'm about to give you. But before you commit to the great trade show adventure, you need to know two things:

1. *Your idea must be protected with at least a PPA.* If it's not, the trade show route is not for you. It would be like putting a bucket of chum on a buffet table for sharks and then being shocked when it gets gobbled up.

2. *Trade shows take time, effort, and money.* They require a lot of preparation and follow-up, and they are not cheap. Still, in terms of bang for your buck, trade shows have my enthusiastic thumbs-up. I'd rather budget for a trade show—where I know the right people will be milling around—than

shell out big bucks for advertising that may or may not even reach my target audience.

Why do one? Because trade shows are teeming with opportunities for pitching to and schmoozing with exactly the right people: those who might license, manufacture, or buy your product. I've met important business contacts there, gotten major press coverage, won Top Ten Product awards, and attracted licensees and buyers. No, not every show is going to be great for everyone, but they are hotbeds of opportunity; you never know who will show up looking for your exact product. Plus the experience is invaluable, since you will be right there alongside some of the most important and successful people in your industry. And it doesn't hurt that trade shows include a lot of vacation-like elements.

Trade Show Tips and Shortcuts

Here are some great tips I've learned in my years of doing trade shows, and I'm passing them along to you so the whole experience is easier and more fun:

■ Start budgeting now: the trade show experience for the big shows comes with a hefty price tag. For starters, it costs a minimum of $1,000 to register for the smallest booth space at most of them. Some places will throw in one table free, especially if you're a first-timer, but others won't (see "Setting Up Your Booth" later in this chapter). You also have to budget in your travel fees, hotel, and meals. I live in the Boston area, so you'd better believe that I maximize every Boston trade show, since it means I'll be saving on airfare. You might want to check out the shows happening near you and practice there before you spend the money to fly off to the other side of the country. To find out where the trade shows are, search online under the category of your product. (For instance, I would search "baby products trade show" or "pet products trade show.") Read the articles and comments about each one. You can also ask store buyers which ones they go to, and which ones they recommend. If you're going to go to all the trouble and expense, you should attend the most popular and reputable one in your particular industry.

■ Each trade show has its own rules, which will be sent to you beforehand. You'll want to read them carefully.

■ Factor in the cost of a friend or relative to help you out. Trade shows are a lot of work for one person, and you never want to leave your booth unattended. You will need to get lunch or take the occasional bathroom break—and of course that will be just the time when someone important will come by! Taking a friend to a trade show may cost a little money, but you can use some of the time to catch up and have fun together. Although many of us can't afford to pay helpers or cover their airfare, you can probably fund their hotel and some meals. I used to invite my best friend from childhood and my sisters to join me, and as our kids got older, my husband would come along. Last year my oldest daughter came to one of the shows (note: kids have to be at least 16 or 18, depending on the show). In every case, we all had a blast and I appreciated the help immensely. Keep in mind that many trade shows take place in tourist destination spots in order to attract attendees, so a fair amount of sightseeing after hours can be included as incentive. Make it sound like so much fun they can't resist going. One of my sisters is always asking me when the next trade show is scheduled!

■ Be curious and convivial, and have fun chatting with people. Sometimes you'll meet someone mutually beneficial, or make new friends. In fact, you wouldn't believe some of the interesting characters I've run into

at trade shows. Just be aware that everybody is pretty uptight on day one, tight-lipped and uncommunicative and all business. But by day two, everybody has loosened up and become best buddies, sharing lunch and stories and business contacts. So do walk around and get a good look at the competition, and approach people who might license your product—you may have talked to some of them when you were making your cold calls—but wait until the second or third day to do it. When you do, remember that this personal contact could make a huge difference.

■ Take lots of photos and/or videos of you in your booth, and of fun show events, and especially of important people who drop by your booth. You'd better believe I got lots of great photos of the people from the *Tonight Show*, and of Mrs. Fields, when they stopped by. Put those photos on your social media sites to generate buzz, and get the photos up on your website, which should include an Event or Media tab (see Chapter 16). Photos of you in your booth, with or without famous people, give you credibility with licensees and buyers. It shows them that you're serious about your product and willing to put in the extra time, effort, and expense to promote it.

■ Attend the industry party. The big, important trade shows always include one, and it's a fun way to meet more people. Yes, it costs extra, but the more people you can interface with, the better your chances of selling your product. Just be sure not to overdo it and start swinging off the chandeliers, because that would give the wrong impression. We're trying to look professional here! Still, you can make some very friendly connections once everybody has had a drink or three.

■ Carry your business cards with you everywhere you go, even to the bathroom, and hand them out to everyone who seems interested.

■ Collect business cards and flyers from everyone, especially those who visit your booth, and scribble notes on the back to jog your memory later. Be sure to organize them once you're back at the hotel every night. You may think you'll remember who's who when you get home, but chances are you'll hit information overload instead. And you will want to follow up on lots of them!

■ You'll receive a show directory when you register. Keep it; it's a goldmine of possible future contacts.

■ Look at the show as an excuse for extra fun. Of course I had to shop for cowboy boots when I was in Dallas, and I surprised my husband at a Vegas trade show one year by booking a tacky chapel and renewing our wedding vows. "Elvis" was our preacher.

What to Bring or Do Before the Show

Preparation makes all the difference:

■ Take along lots of your beefed-up sell sheets and business cards.

■ Every major trade show has a press room where people from the media can get information about the attendees. You need to make and bring with you at least two dozen copies, more or less, depending on the size of the show, of something called a press kit (see sidebar), which you will leave in the press room. Each one is organized in an envelope or folder, on the front of which is your product name, an illustration or photo and/or your subject line, and your booth number. Some people even include a sample product with their press kit. You want to snag the media's interest so they'll write about you and your product, or interview you right at your booth!

While there's usually a copy center on site so you can make more press kits if you have to, it's better to bring more than you think you'll need, if you can fit them in your luggage.

■ Depending on how tech savvy you are, you can do what a lot of companies have been doing lately—create electronic press kits that are available (and strategically placed) on your website. It could conceivably be cheaper than having the convention hall's copy center make copies, it's environmentally conscious, and if you ever run out of physical copies, you can always direct people toward the website for more information. In most cases, potential customers and the media would be stopping at your website anyway. Just be sure that you have tons of business cards with your website and contact information on them! In fact, printing out business cards sometimes can be cheaper than printing out press releases.

What's a Press Kit?

A good press kit includes a press release about your product, a good photo of it, your business card, your sell sheet, and any other promotional materials you have.

■ Usually the big shows will write a press release on their letterhead and will send it to your local papers so they can hype you and your idea in your surrounding area.

■ Invite contacts to come see you at the show. It adds luster to you and your product.

■ It's best to have a sample of an actual product to display and demon-strate. If you're making the product yourself, but you're not in full produc-tion yet, do a "short run" (just a few pieces) for the show, if you can, and bring them. Just be sure that you'll be able to fill the orders that come in from folks you meet. (See Chapter 14.)

■ It doesn't hurt to have a demo video shown in your booth. Most con-vention centers will let you rent audio/visual equipment during the trade show, but like a lot of the costs of attending a trade show, it can be expen-sive. If you have enough tech knowledge, you can connect your laptop to their audio/visual equipment. If it's too complicated for you, you can al-ways have the video playing on your laptop or tablet. Although the venue will make you pay for electricity, you can charge your laptop in your hotel room at night. If you don't want to lug your computer around, show them the demo on your phone. But the best thing is to do a live demo right there.

■ Bring things you can ditch after the show so your return trip is lighter. For instance, I bought four mannequin heads to display my Hat Wrap. They were cheap but not all that easy to pack, so I gave them the heave-ho after the show. If you've gotten to the stage of having actual products, sell them at the end so you don't have to drag them back with you. Even better, you'll have some cash in your pocket.

■ Consider printing T-shirts with your logo and product name on the front and your web address on the back, for you and your helper/s to wear. You can do this inexpensively online or through your graphic artist. I started out with inexpensive one-color designs to fit my lean budget, but once I got successful, I could spring for fancy embroidered shirts. This is trade show couture: almost everyone will be wearing a special shirt.

■ Everybody loves freebies, so be sure to have pens, key chains, or thumb drives with your product name and/or website printed on them (you can get these very inexpensively online) to give out. Or if you want to do this really cheaply, just fill a bowl of candy and give it out with a business card. And be sure to collect a stash of stuff from the other attendees to take back to your kids or friends.

■ Office supplies are essential: order sheets, pens, pencils, a sturdy stapler, scissors, tape, extra paper.

■ Breath mints and snacks can save your skin—sometimes you really can't leave your booth for hours, and you won't want to.

Setting Up Your Booth

Making a booth look fancy is big business. Some moneyed companies ship in their booth components a few days early, then fly in a whole crew to set it up. Sure, those booths look phenomenal, but I can set up in under an hour and attract the same buyers. In fact, to my eye, some of the more elaborate booths make the products look lost or small.

Basically, it's all a racket: because you can't lug chairs, plush carpet, fancy table drapery, or even a wastebasket on the plane with you, you have to rent or buy it all there, and it isn't cheap. In fact, that's how the trade show organizers make a lot of their money, and they may try to convince you to rent or buy a lot of stuff you don't really need. Just remember that the buyers and licensees strolling by your booth are interested in your product, not the stage setting, so as long as yours looks professional, you can save money and do it simply. I've learned to pack very, very lightly: one rolling bag holds the clothes I need plus all the materials for setting up my simple but sleek booth.

Be sure not to book your return flight too early, because you will be penalized if you take down your booth before the closing time.

Money-Saving Hints

Because we're not made of money:

■ Shop for the lowest prices among the hotels listed in the pre-show brochure. If you're worried about getting to the show from your inexpensive hotel, you can relax. The fact that the hotel was listed in the brochure means there will probably be a free shuttle bus that you can take to get to the show. When I was just starting out, I could barely afford to stay in the cheapest hotel, but I imagined being so successful someday that I could stay in the swanky hotel where the trade show actually took place—and my dream eventually came true. This visualization stuff really works, so try it!

■ A table to hold your product and a plastic stand to hold your sell sheets and business cards may be all you need. You can buy the plastic stand at an office supply store and bring it with you. It's worth it to buy or rent basic table skirts at the show to hide what's underneath your table if they're not thrown in free.

■ You will need a sign or two, but you can work with your local sign company or graphic artist to come up with a fairly inexpensive vinyl sign to roll up and bring with you as well. This is an investment that you'll use over and over. Remember that your sign will be the first thing to catch anyone's eye, so it has to be something compelling to bring people to your booth.

■ Instead of renting a chair, I would sit on my rolling carry-on luggage if

I got tired. When you're not sitting on it, you can stash it under your table. The truth is, you'll be standing most of the time, so comfortable shoes are a must.

■ I use double-sided tape or string to hang my vinyl sign rather than investing in expensive hangers.

■ You don't need to order carpeting. Just wear your comfortable shoes and place your table in front lengthwise so nobody sees the floor.

■ Why rent an overpriced wastebasket when you can use a plastic bag and hide it under your table?

■ Just remember that you're at the trade show to meet people who might buy your product, to see what others are doing in your field, to make connections—and to have fun.

■ Once you get home, you will want to organize all of the possible contacts you made and follow up with e-mails and calls, reminding them that you met at the trade show. If you were lucky enough to get orders, you'll need to get busy filling them. And if you got a licensee, you'll start the process of finalizing a licensing agreement.

Trade shows can be the start of something very big.

OTHER OPPORTUNITIES TO PITCH IT

It doesn't stop with trade shows: you just need a little imagination to find venues for letting the public know that you and your product exist. For instance, when I was promoting my Parachute Dog pet waste disposal kit, I went to a Paws 4 A Cure event, a walkathon that raises funds for animals in need of medical help. Tables for events like these are usually reasonably priced, and you meet a lot of people whose area of interest coincides with your product. I brought samples with me, and gave them out. People were hooked, and bought them once they'd used their sample. Because of the Paws 4 A Cure event, I was invited to be part of a dog photography event put on by the same organization, where I had another table and sold even more.

Sometimes, if your press release generates enough buzz, you can get invited to speak about your product at a meeting or convention. The National Highway Traffic Safety Administration invited me to show my car seat mirror as a nice solution to the front seat airbag problem.

When the Moms In Business Unite conference asked me to do a session on cashing in on your "aha" moments, I brought the Parachute Dog kit with me. It was voted Best New Product of the Year at the conference, which meant more great kudos to mention in press releases and on my website.

Likewise, I was invited to show my product at an event held at the State House in Boston by the Center for Women & Enterprise, to show my support for state funding encouraging women entrepreneurs. I actually spoke with a Massachusetts senator—and the governor—about the importance of such programs. Your own local government is just waiting for you to get involved, and it's a great photo op.

I like to attend invention conventions at local schools, because I love to

see what the next generation is coming up with and because teaching and inspiring others is my passion.

Then there is InnovationNights.com. This great concept originated in Massachusetts, and is really catching on. Basically, it's a free launch party and live networking event, an opportunity for you to pitch your product and get featured on social media all over. When my product was featured at a Mass Innovation Nights event, it generated so much buzz that the president of the Inventors' Association of New England invited me to speak at MIT. It's a great way to promote your idea totally free, and a perfect place to make helpful contacts.

Be a Media Maven

You might be surprised at the national and local radio and television stations, newspapers, magazines, websites, and blogs that will be interested in you and your product—and mentions from these media can snowball into international attention. If your brilliant press releases manage to snag an appearance for you, go for it!

Radio shows are a great way to go, since they're usually done live on the phone, which means you don't have any travel expenses. My press release about Parachute Dog resulted in a lot of radio airtime, which translated into inquiries and sales.

When I was invited to be on a popular live television talk show, of course I went, even though I'd never done anything like it before and it was a little daunting. They were doing a question-and-answer segment on inventing, and I was the token inventor. They had also invited a prominent patent attorney. Talk about distracting! Bright lights, a strange studio setting—not to mention a plug in my ear, and we'd gotten lost on the way to the studio so I missed my hair and makeup session, and there was no way to really prep my answers because it was call-in. But I realized all I had to do was find my voice with each question, smile, and enjoy the experience. The attorney was nervous and actually deferred a lot of questions to me, and he wasn't smiling much, either. The segment was so successful that it ran much longer than planned—and when I saw it onscreen, I realized that my smile made me look pleasant, self-confident, and completely at ease.

When you're asked about your product, just give 'em the pitch and let your enthusiasm for your brainchild shine. And smile!

Paid Advertising

It's not much of a stretch from a sell sheet or a press release to an eye-catching ad. There are even ways you can barter for ad space in local periodicals—by writing an article on your area of expertise, for instance (because, remember, they're constantly looking for great new copy).

It pays to be imaginative here, too: I paid for an ad and order form for the car seat mirror to be placed in New Mom maternity packets in hospitals and maternity centers, which generated a lot of sales before the product was widely distributed in stores. This was a great target audience, too, because new parents quickly realized the need to be able to see their infant when the baby was facing the wrong way in the back seat, so they ordered the mirror. Those sales led to mail-order catalogs—which led to more store orders and then to a licensee and even wider distribution than I could have dreamed of on my own.

You could hire a publicist to find you radio and television speaking gigs and appearances, but the cost is often prohibitive. If you put the work in, you can function as your own publicist, especially with your social media (see Chapter 16).

Another possibility is to make a direct-response TV commercial, but you may want to consider it carefully before jumping in. In the days before the Internet, I made one. It was a 30-second professional-looking ad for my car seat mirror that a company wrote and edited, and a crew taped on my side street, using my sister and niece as actors. It was like one of those "As Seen on TV" commercials with a toll-free number to order and everything. I loved the project, thinking it was a great way to demonstrate the product to the masses—remember, this was prior to the Internet—but it cost a lot of money and I also had to buy airtime. It turned out that the only airtime I could afford was when most people were asleep, so nobody saw it. What a waste! Today, I would never pay a company up front to do this kind of commercial, because there are some that will expect payment only if your product sells. Plus I have the option now of doing it all online.

The biggest news in the DIY advertising world is the Internet: You can get incredible advertising deals through Facebook and other social media sites. I'll be telling you how to build your online platform and use the power of the web to promote your products in Chapter 16.

Free Advertising

Technology has changed the need for expensive and untargeted advertising. It's amazing that today you can shoot a "commercial" on your phone, edit it, and send it out through your social media *free*. You can have your own channel on YouTube and target your ads to appropriate audiences, with all the research done for you. You don't want to miss this wave, believe me—and it's crazy easy. Free advertising through e-mail also is a great way to go. There's more about both of these methods in Chapter 16.

My husband and I would wear my Hat Wrap everywhere we went with our infants in their backpacks—but especially to children's events and the Children's Museum. We always got lots of interest and people wanting to know where to get one of their own. You can do something like this, too;

use your product in heavily trafficked areas where people will see it and be curious and impressed.

If your product isn't overly expensive, and you have the inventory, give out samples instead of paying for expensive advertising! When we take Coconut to the dog park, I take samples with me. People inevitably see us using the Parachute Dog kit and love it. I also put samples and order forms at all the local veterinarians' offices. Just consider handing out samples another form of advertising—and it's very effective. Never underestimate the ripples-in-the-stream effect.

No matter what I'm giving away, I always make sure to include my website so people can order more.

Now that you've developed your pitch, and people are interested, you're ready to go on to the chapter that will help you make a big decision— should I manufacture my product myself, or keep looking for a licensee? If you decide to build an empire, I'll show you the ins and outs of starting your own business around your idea, including several unconventional ways to get funding for it. If you decide to keep pursuing the licensing route, I'll tell you what you need to know about licensing agreements. And just to let you know, even though some inventing gurus out there suggest that those who just want to be idea people should quit if they don't find a licensee right off the bat, and go on to another idea, just remember that if I had done that, I wouldn't be where I am today. So even if you're ready to throw in the towel, read the next chapter.

Make It (Step Five)

Factory in the Kitchen (or Not)

Alice came to a fork in the road. "Which road do I take?" she asked.

"Where do you want to go?" responded the Cheshire Cat.

"I don't know," Alice answered.

"Then," said the Cat, "it doesn't matter."

—LEWIS CARROLL

This chapter is about an important question that every inventor needs to answer (unless you want to sell your idea outright for a lump sum): Do I try to find a licensee to make and sell my product for royalties, or do I do it myself? To make sure you don't end up like Alice in Wonderland, it helps to know where you want to go—but when it comes to the licensing versus building a business adventure, you may end up in a place you didn't expect, even if you think you know where you want to go. I know I did. I had been selling a product on my own for five years and my business was growing when I unexpectedly heard from a very eager licensee. I decided to go with that company, which took my product to a whole new level. It soared into bestseller territory and my future was changed for the better.

LICENSING

Finding an established, reputable company to license your product is the greatest way to go, since there is very little risk to you; the company takes it all on and you just get paid. The catch is finding a licensee, which can take a very long time indeed, if it happens at all. And even if you do find one, sometimes you end up having to license to another company because something isn't working out with the first one.

In this section, I'll tell you some important things to know that will help you make the best choices when it comes to licensees. You'll get the skinny on licensing agents, go through the basics of the all-important license agreement so it will make sense to you, and will find out about one of the great perks that comes along with finding a licensee.

Licensing Agents: What Are They? Do I Need One?

Licensing agents make their money by matching your product with potential licensees. If they're successful and a deal is reached, they make a percentage, usually 5 to 10 percent of what you make, but this can vary depending on the service they provide.

I tried this route, and it turns out the agent I hired contacted one business. One! Good grief, I could do better than that on an off day. And that one company didn't even go for it. I decided then and there that I'd keep the percentage, thanks, and contact potential licensees myself. Of course, you may get lucky and find an agent who will work their fingers to the bone for you, or has the perfect connections, but my theory is that nobody will work as hard for your idea as you will.

Product submission or search companies are another form of a middleman offering to find you a licensee, but they present hazards of their own (see sidebar).

Finding a Licensee

I gave you the basics of finding a licensee in Chapter 11, so you may want to take another look at that. Also, I will give you step-by-step instructions on how to find a potential licensee through LinkedIn in Chapter 16. Remember that a mid-size company may do better by you and your product because it has more resources, time, and attention to devote to you. Big companies are often spread very thinly over a wide range of products so you don't get the individual attention, and they're often mired in bureaucracy. But some big companies may prove to be the exception to the rule, so don't dismiss one if it comes your way.

A Word of Warning

Online product submission companies have become very popular, and you always have the option of pitching or submitting your idea to one of them. There are many different models out there, but most of them are middlemen that match inventors with companies looking for a particular type of new idea, claiming that they try to match potential licensees to you. They are very enticing to inventors because they're new, they're easy, and some don't even require a product; all you need is an idea. Most make their money by charging a submission fee and then, if you do get a deal, taking a chunk of the royalties. All of this is outlined in lengthy legalese that you must agree to prior to submitting. The tricky thing is that in many cases the company you're dealing with will own the patent—and I feel that there's no reason for anyone but you to own your patent in any licensing deal.

I did go through a couple of the online companies myself, before I realized that they would own my patent as part of the deal. I read a lot of complaints online after the fact. So then I was left wondering, What if the company goes bankrupt? Where does my patent go? I've learned since then that they're really only doing what you could do perfectly well on your own: looking for a company to sell your product. And how do you know they're even demonstrating your product correctly?

I think you can tell that I'm not a big fan of this approach, partly because I've learned that there's no magic company that will do something you couldn't do yourself. If you do the very same legwork, you get to keep more of the profits as well as ownership of your intellectual property. And then there's the sleaze factor; some of these companies are downright unscrupulous. So you need to know what you're getting into and what you might be giving up.

If you're considering product submission or product search sites, inventor assistance sites, or product evaluation companies, do yourself a favor and first search the company name with the word "complaints" after it, and read everything about it. Then you can make an informed decision.

There is also such a thing as in-person product searches. You usually hear about these online, on TV, or in magazines. They involve traveling to a destination and spending a whole day in a room filled with hundreds of other inventors, all of you just waiting to give your pitch to a guru of one kind or another, hoping they like you enough to license you. In some cases you make a second cut, which means you have to come back for another whole day—and even then chances are you won't get the deal. Although these in-person events do still exist, most product searches are done online now, and I have to say, that's a good thing. The in-person searches tend to be exhausting, expensive, and disappointing for most of the participants. However, as I learned through experience, the online searches have many downsides too. You most likely will be better off keeping your money in your pocket and doing the work yourself.

The License Agreement

So, your product caught a licensee! You deserve huge congratulations. Now you need to negotiate your way through a crucial legal document: the license agreement.

Usually, you will hash out the basic details (like the percentage of royalties you'll be making) on the phone. Once those basics are hammered out, the licensee will send you a copy of the agreement. After you receive it you can either negotiate some more or sign it if it's to your liking.

Because every deal is different and I'm not a lawyer, I'm not going to include a generic agreement here for you to fill in the blanks. What I will do, though, is explain what you should look for, request, and demand in order to get the best deal. Remember that most agreements are furnished by the licensee, and they are mostly on the up and up, but you must always go over the document very carefully to be sure you're being given a fair deal.

A license agreement is meant to give both you and the licensing company legal protection. The following are some of the important and often negotiable points that you will usually find included in an agreement:

Royalties. Royalties are what you'll be getting paid. They're a percentage of the net selling price of each item sold, and they usually range from 3 to 10 percent. When you're in the negotiation phase of your agreement, you should start high and expect them to come down a little. The agreement should state that you'll get paid a royalty as long as the company is making and selling your idea or product. Make sure that your agreement includes royalties for any country the company sells it in, even though you don't have foreign patents. You also have the option to keep it as U.S. sales and royalties only (if you have other interest from licensees outside the United States). Also included will be the timing of your royalty payments. These are often paid quarterly, on or before the 15th of the month following the close of the preceding calendar quarter. The royalties should be accompanied by a report showing the number of products sold, the net selling price for each customer during the preceding quarter, and the amount of royalty due. The licensee is expected to keep accurate and complete books, and you or a representative should be able to inspect the books relating to your product at suitable intervals after you give a reasonable notice that you want to do so.

Start Date. You'll want to be sure the agreement includes a reasonable date when the product will be ready to sell (you don't want your darling brainchild sitting around on ice forever).

Minimums. This specifies the minimum number of your products that the company must sell in the first year (and the amount of royalties that would generate). If the minimums aren't met, the licensee must make up the difference in a dollar amount. In other words, if the royalties paid for any calendar year do not equal the minimum dollar amount, the licensee pays you the difference, usually no later than 30 days after the end of the calendar year. This guarantees performance on the licensee's part, since you don't want someone licensing your product and then not producing it—especially since that would mean you're stuck and can't get out of the deal. You may increase the minimum as your product begins to sell over the years, so this number can be a sliding or adjustable one. Remember that the licensee is investing a lot in your product, so you don't want to be too greedy. To arrive at a fair minimum during the negotiation phase, ask how many the company expects to sell in the first year and/or in which stores. If the company tells you it will get your product into ABC Store, search online as soon as you hang up to see how many stores ABC has, and base your minimum on the facts. For example, if ABC has 200 stores, and each store sells three of your products per week (a very conservative estimate), that translates to 31,200 units. If your royalty rate is 10 percent of a net selling price of $5, your minimum would be $15,600.00. If the licensee comes up short, it would have to pay you the difference in order to keep the agreement in force.

Exclusive vs. Non-Exclusive. "Exclusive" means that the licensee is the only company you are allowing to manufacture and sell your product. "Non-exclusive" means you can license it with other companies. Naturally most deals will be exclusive. Keep in mind that you can specify what market or category the licensee can sell it in. For example, if I licensed my mirror to a company that had absolutely no ties to automotive stores, I could state that lack of ties in the agreement and then be free to also license it to a company that did have automotive ties. Protect yourself against missed opportunities—be sure your licensee has ability and history in all the categories that apply.

Term. This specifies how long the agreement is in force. Some inventors sign a two-year agreement with the intention to reassess for a longer term at the end of that period. Others keep it in force for as long as the products

are being sold. If the product is patented, the agreement may expire when the patent does. For design patents, the term is 14 years, and there are no maintenance fees required. The term for utility patents is 20 years from the filing date, but no less than 17 years—assuming the holder pays the required maintenance fees at the 4-, 8-, and 12-year points.

Modifications Clause. This states that even if modifications or changes are made to your product, you'll still get royalties. This is pretty crucial: you don't want a company making a teeny tweak to your idea and then saying it doesn't need to pay you because of the change. Also, you want to be sure that any improvements, modifications, and substitutions during the term of the agreement will belong to you.

Advance. This is an amount paid to you upon signing the agreement, and it's usually deducted from future royalties. It's not too common, so don't be surprised if it isn't offered to you. While it would be nice to get an advance, it's not a deal-breaker if you don't.

Liability Policy. Suppose somebody loses an eye flipping the cap off your gizmo. They'll sue. You want to be sure you're covered by the licensee's policy with a legitimate insurance carrier that's acceptable to you, and that the licensee will name you as one of the insured. Make sure the limit is high (for instance, some agreements specify that the limit be no less than $3 million).

Performance. This is where the licensee could list any trade shows the company will be attending, or other ways it will promote your product. It's nice, for instance, to know that your licensee is going to showcase your product at an international trade show. But this clause is not that common, so it's not a deal-breaker if it's not included.

Quality. Be sure to specify that the quality of your product must meet an agreed-upon design. This will protect you against the possibility of shoddy production.

Trademark Rights. If you've already trademarked an aspect of your product, you'll need to grant the licensee the rights to use it, if it wants to. The company might even pay you money for it!

Patent. It is ideal for you to retain your patent even if the licensee is paying the legal fees for it, so look very carefully at the language around patent ownership.

Indemnification. This extra layer of protection should be included, but it's so complicated that you will probably need your attorney to review it for you.

Termination Agreement. It's a good idea for both parties to have an out, as long as you feel it's fair to you. Have the attorney check the language.

Once you understand all the terms, and if you like what you see in your agreement, ask your attorney to take a look at it. You don't need the attorney to pore over it for hours and hours (at the usual stiff hourly rate). Just tell her or him you're happy with it, and ask to be alerted if anything looks screamingly wrong with it, or if there's something unique to your situation that needs to be added. Hopefully the attorney will tell you it looks great and that you can go ahead and sign it.

Now that the agreement is signed, the real fun begins. There's nothing more exciting than seeing the licensee's version of your product—and receiving royalty checks that go on getting fatter and fatter!

The Special Perk of Having a Licensee

Once you have a licensee and things are going well, the company may ask you for other ideas. These ideas can be presented much less formally than your original. I was able to get other ideas licensed and patented with simple drawings, photos, or verbal descriptions (although you'll want to always document and protect yourself through NDAs and paper trails). This is great for both parties, and it's so much fun pumping out ideas and seeing them produced.

BUILDING YOUR OWN BUSINESS

Sure, getting a licensee for your product is a great way to go, but sometimes it just doesn't happen, and that can be a big disappointment. Then again, I've always thought that what looks like a door closing can actually be the opening of a great window of opportunity—so if it's taking too long to find a licensee, or if you have exhausted your list of possibilities, and you know for sure that your product is marketable, then why not think about starting your own business? Let me tell you, it's great to be the one calling the shots! You can decide to make your company as big or as small as you like; you can just sell through your website, do house parties, sell only in specialty stores, or in catalogs, or you can go big. All at your own pace.

Ever since I was 15, I knew I wanted my own business. Even when I was working at my lowly summer jobs I was constantly taking notes because I knew I could do it better (or at least do it my way) when that big day came. I always thought it would be cool to be my own boss, and I wanted to be a really good one to my employees (especially when I didn't like the boss I had at the time!). Maybe it had something to do with my upbringing, because my mother was always telling me how great business-owners' life-styles were. Whatever the reason, I decided very early on that I wanted to be the owner of wherever I was working.

You may decide to build a business, too. Starting your own business is exciting—and a little daunting—but never boring.

Let's start with seven of the most common misconceptions.

1. *I don't have the skills to start a business.* Anyone who knows how to keep track of their home expenses, keep a budget, and pay bills has business skills. And if you are a parent, you're probably managing a million and one things: cell phones, sports, Girl Scout cookies, paper routes, medical appointments, managing the house, shopping, and on and on. All of your organizational abilities translate into business abilities. I once heard someone say that the average mom could be a two-star general because of everything she has to manage!

2. *I should get investors for my business.* If your product is extremely complex or costly to produce, you will probably need to get investors of some sort. But if your product is fairly simple, you should probably avoid taking on investors. Certainly, if you get investors at least you're not putting your own money on the line, which is why many people are big fans of the idea. But I'm not. Why? Because if you have investors, then your investors own you—which pretty much kills the idea of being your own boss. Call it Yankee pride or independence, but I'd rather keep the control myself. I've started all my companies on a shoestring, but I was able to feed them as they grew.

In fact, I love the whole concept of "bootstrapping," or pulling yourself up by your own bootstraps, without outside help in the form of loans or investors. When I was just starting up my own business, I asked my brother-in-law Rick—who was pretty high up in the financial world—if he had any helpful connections for me. He told me the best advice he had was to "bootstrap" so that I wouldn't have to pay anyone back. At the time I was perturbed that he wasn't putting me in touch with any generous, wealthy moguls (I assumed there was a secret network of them somewhere). My dad had taught me how to golf as a young kid because he said a lot of business deals were made there and it was important for girls to learn this sport, and I was looking forward to striking a deal on the golf course! But no. Now, looking back, I realize that Rick was right and it was really good advice. I would tell you to do the same. I reap every penny my products make, since nobody is waiting for repayment. It's a good way to go if you can swing it. In fact, one of the biggest pitfalls that entrepreneurs fall into is getting into massive debt, borrowing too much, and sinking under the burden.

The exception to this if-they-invest-they-own-you concept is the new phenomenon of crowdfunding, where you put out a call for contributions, and independent donors give money, no strings attached. I think is a great option for inventors, rather than getting a loan or stakeholder investors. There are several such sites: Kickstarter was one of the first, but if you don't make your target goal amount in the time allotted, you don't receive a single penny of the donations that people pledged. You may also want to check out Indiegogo.com, FundaGeek.com, or awesomefoundation.org. They all have different rules and parameters. I think if this option had been around when I first started, I would have given it a try.

I must say, though, that just because you get a hunk of money from some outside source doesn't mean you'll automatically know how to spend it wisely or well. I think if you're using your own money, you'll be more prudent, at least in the beginning!

3. *I'll have more free time.* Sorry folks, but that's just not true: *all* of your time and energy will go into your company. It's a bit like raising a baby,

since your business will need constant nurturing and dedication, and sometimes you'll even suffer sleep deprivation. But keep in mind that your invention is *your* baby and nobody else's, and it's a great pleasure to see it thrive and grow. And as for working all those extra hours, if you're like me, business is enjoyment, so it won't really feel like work. And you can make your hours completely flexible.

4. *I'll get rich quick.* If you are doing this business-building thing to make a million in no time, think again. As soon as you make money it needs to go right back into the business in order for it to survive and grow. Yes, the potential exists to make a lot of money, but creating a firm foundation for your eventual success is a process. Just pay yourself a little at a time, and put off buying your Maserati for a while. Also, it's wise to keep a nice fat piggy bank for legal expenses, just in case, because once your product starts selling well, the copycats may follow.

5. *I should hire my friends and relatives and/or get their financial support.* It's crucial to get the *emotional* support of your partner, family, or friends, and if they want to help you do some of the grunt work of assembly and packaging, that's fine too. In fact, I've thrown some great assembly-line parties and everyone had a great time while we got some products assembled. But getting professional business or financial support from friends or family? Not a good idea, unless you want to run the risk of ruining your friendships or starting a family feud. Just as they say you should never lend money to a friend or relation, it's safer to hire outside help and minimize the chances of disappointment, hurt, or blame.

6. *I need to give up my day job if I start a business.* No you don't—in fact, having the cushion of your day-job income (and health insurance!) is a good thing. When I first started out as a freelance graphic designer, I was still

working full time at my job. I met clients at a local café or at their offices, before and after my regular work hours—and my hourly rate was five times what I made at my job, so there was real incentive to go independent. I waited, though, until I had the equipment I needed, had connected with the right contacts, and was making some serious money on my own—and then, off I went. I've never regretted it. But I waited until it was the right time.

7. I've had friends who complain bitterly about their parent or partner who has their own business. Isn't it a pain? I've known some complainers myself, but the actual owner of the business seemed to be having a blast, even though they were relentlessly bugged around the clock with problems and questions. When you build a business around your own invention, it's just an extension of the process you've already accomplished, a way to see it to fruition. You've created it, and creating anything is exciting. Starting a business is just another kind of inventing—only what you're inventing now is a business to showcase your invention! But in the final analysis, the only person who can really know if you have the personality, passion, and commitment to build your own business is you. To me, building a business is just another form of the inventing process—and I love it.

Common Questions

Here are the answers to some common questions about building your own business:

What kind of business should I have? There are different ways to set up a business: sole proprietorship, limited liability company (LLC), corporation (Inc.), and more. Before you decide which kind of business will be the best for you, talk to the person who will be a valued member of your team: a good local accountant, especially one who is expert at business law, since every state has different laws and requirements. Your accountant will advise you as you grow. How to find one? References and Internet comments will help.

In most cases, you will need to set up a business banking account with a checking account and perhaps a credit card in your business name. Look for free checking with no minimums.

Do I need a business plan? Investors will expect to see one, but if you're boot-strapping, the way I did, or looking into crowdfunding, you don't need a specific plan—you just need a compelling vision. I'm not a big advocate of planning out every single detail, because being an entrepreneur means you're forging a new path, which means the future is pretty much unknown and unpredictable. I'd rather be flexible, responding to each scenario as it unfolds. I've found it helpful to think in 6- to 12-month chunks, and to come up with solutions to possible problems. Doing that allows you to nip trouble in the bud. Keep in mind that large businesses move at a glacial pace and have to plan with years of future in mind. The beauty of a smaller business like yours is that you can respond quickly and immediately, jumping in on opportunities faster.

What about sales and marketing? Your social media can be your headquarters for most of your marketing and public relations, as you'll learn in Chapter 16. If you have a good online platform, you may not need traditional salespeople. You'll probably be your own best salesperson, at least in the beginning, because no one will know your product like you do, or be as enthusiastic about it as you are. However, if you get so busy that you need help, you may want to hire a sales representative. You can find one by asking store owners who they use, or you can general-search. Because store

buyers and owners like to see several products at once (they're busy!), a sales rep who brings several products to the table is more likely to get in the door. You and your rep will need to sign a short contract spelling out the agreement, but reps usually make around 15 percent commission on your sales. This may not be affordable if your profit margins are tight. The good news, though, is that in this age of technology, store owners are more open to dealing directly with you, and because they have access to demo videos and your website, you don't have to show up in person.

Do I need liability insurance? Yes. All you need is for someone to misuse your product and end up suffering some kind of injury—and then suing you for every asset you've got. You should ask your patent attorney, accountant, and/or insurance agent for advice. Get quotes from reputable insurance agencies that carry product liability policies. These are usually paid quarterly and run a few hundred dollars per quarter, depending on the product. It's also important to put warnings on the product and packaging. For instance, I always include a suffocation warning about the plastic bags that are part of my dog waste cleanup kit.

What are my options for accepting payment? Of course, cash is always good, and checks are fine for store orders if that's in accordance with your payment terms (payment up front on delivery of product is usual, or payment in thirty days is also common). Also, since many of us sell through our websites, setting up a PayPal account makes sense and it's easy to do. People trust PayPal, so they feel secure using it. If you do sell at events or mobile pop-up shops, be sure to get a credit card reader through PayPal Here (www.paypalhere.com) or a service such as Square (www.squareup.com). The reader attaches to your phone and makes sales super-easy anywhere you go. More than likely, there'll be more companies that provide similar products and services in the future.

Do I need employees? It all depends on how big your business is. It makes sense for small-business owners to hire freelancers as needed, rather than going through the hassle of hiring employees and dealing with taxes, worker's comp, and all the rest of it. You can put ads in your local paper, or go through a website like HireMyMom.com, Elance.com, or Craigslist.org. Just make sure to have written agreements in place.

What do you recommend for shipping? This is a no-brainer: the good old U.S. Postal Service is easy, convenient, and the supplies are free! You can even have your packages picked up at your door. Priority mail is guaranteed quick delivery, and if your product fits into one of their flat-rate free boxes, it's reasonably priced. You can print out a label on your computer and pay for the whole process online—you don't have to go to the post office at all.

Should I rent office space? Having a home office really lowers the overhead, and that's how many of us start out. But sometimes it's too hard to work at home. Once you can afford it, having an outside office that you either share with one other person or have all to yourself is a wonderful luxury. After my days of using the local Starbucks or library for my free office—or my basement or kitchen—I eventually rented an office space downtown. And you don't need to go nuts buying expensive office furniture—I got mine free or used: a file cabinet, a desk that somebody was getting rid of, and a display area to showcase my products. Being a visual learner, I brought in a painter's easel with some paints and a couple of whiteboards for visually mapping it out so I could "think" things through, and I had a dartboard for important decision making (so much more exciting than flipping a coin). It was someplace I had to get dressed up for and drive to, and somehow that made it feel very official and professional, even though my view overlooked a dumpster and parking lot. It may not have been luxurious, but I still loved it, and I could assemble my products there with no

171

interference from young children. But some of us need to be surrounded by noise and bustle and people, and a quiet office can feel lonely, so it wouldn't really work for them. For instance, Quentin Tarantino wrote some of his screenplays in a busy pie shop, and J.K. Rowling started the Harry Potter series in cafés. A nice compromise is the office "hive" concept, where several people share space. Workbar Boston is one example, but you could general-search the idea to see what's available in your area. There are even shared spaces that offer day care on one side.

Still, it's good to know that you can do the whole office thing for next to nothing. Some days I'd grab a coffee at Starbucks and then take it along with my laptop next door to a cozy restaurant that had a fireplace and Wi-Fi. When I got tired of working, I'd go two doors down to an office supply store and sit in one of the massaging office chairs on display! Then I'd go back to my basement to assemble my orders.

Important Things to Keep in Mind

There's more to running a business than the basics of employees and office space. Be sure you always remember these important points:

Impeccable customer service is key. In fact, great customer service is what will differentiate your company from the rest. Several years ago, I got a call from a woman who told me her car seat mirror was defective, that it was so warped that she couldn't use it and could I send her another one. I was very surprised—and worried—and when I asked what happened, she told me it melted in her dishwasher. When I asked why it was in the dishwasher, she said it was dirty. Even though I was thinking "OMG, this woman has a baby?", I did send her a new one and suggested that she not put this one in the dishwasher. From then on, I included a sticker that said "To clean: wipe with a soft cloth." But a satisfied customer is one who will tell others about your great service.

I sometimes send loyal customers a couple of small freebies in a holiday card, just to say thank you, or I give out a limited supply of fun goodies with each online order from my website—so I'm building my brand with an emotional connection (see Chapter 16). For example, I gave away a chip clip with my website and logo on it, for use with dog treat bags.

And I always make it a point to contact customers promptly if there's a question or a concern.

Stay organized. Most of us have our preferred ways of staying organized. I'm a sticky-note kind of person, but I have friends who keep detailed to-do lists, and others who enter everything into their phones. The method doesn't matter, but the final goal is clarity around what you've done and what still needs to be accomplished! When tax time rolls around, you will also be glad of any filing or collecting of receipts that you've managed to do.

Think outside the box. Here's a great idea: have a mobile pop-up shop, like those food trucks you see parked on roadsides or curbsides all over. You may need special permits, so check with your state or local officials. But once you're legit, you could use Twitter or Facebook to let people know where you'll be showing up, and offer something special to the 10th or 50th person to visit—maybe a free product, special discount, or something fun to entice customers. Choose locations that have something to do with your product (for my waste cleanup kit I went to dog parks and dog walk-athons) or just pick busy spots at random. The portable store is novel and it's a lot of fun. In fact, this alone could be your business model.

Small—and direct—can be beautiful. If you're selling directly to customers online or through pop-up stores or other small venue, you don't need fancy packaging and you make all the profit because you're not selling your product wholesale! Finally the game is going in favor of inventors and small businesses—and someday there may not even be a need for stores or a sales force.

And remember that the game can change! Even though you're manufacturing and selling your product yourself, licensees may be watching you. And the more sales you get, the better deal you can command. Sometimes when you're up to your eyeballs in orders to fill, a company may be preparing a license agreement to offer you that's just too good to refuse. It happened to me, and just in the nick of time—because I was at a crossroads trying to decide whether I wanted to take my business to the next level. So just because you build a business doesn't mean you can't end up with a sweet licensing deal.

MANUFACTURING: OVER THERE, SOMEWHERE HERE, OR DIY?

What springs to mind when you think of trying to manufacture a product yourself? For a lot of us, I'll bet it's the classic candy-factory episode of *I Love Lucy*, with Lucy and Ethel working frantically at a conveyor belt—and when they get behind, they panic and start stuffing candy in their mouths. I guess that falls under the category of any assembly worker's worst nightmare, but having designed my own assembly lines at home, I can tell you that there are lots of reasons why it's great to DIY when it comes to assembling and packaging your product—just as long as the components are within budget and the final product is relatively simple. If your product is complicated, you will probably need to hire an appropriate manufacturer.

When I look back, it's not surprising that I get such a kick out of putting together many of my products myself. Most of the toys I loved as a kid were the ones that made things—like a pretzel factory complete with conveyor belt, a button- or pin-making machine (which combined graphics and manufacturing), and various molds for making shapes with melted plastic.

Then, in high school I worked as an assistant to an engineer. I got to see firsthand the exciting process of people designing at drafting tables and then taking their designs into the machine shop next door, where the drawings became components that were then assembled into a product. The whole thing was fascinating, but I didn't realize at the time that this after-school job would be so helpful later on! It gave me the grounding I needed to put together a product from its parts—and believe me, if a high-schooler can do that, so can you.

But first, let's look at the other options.

Manufacturing Abroad

We all know why so many products are made outside the United States: it's cheaper, at least if you're dealing with huge quantities. But most individual inventors just don't have the resources to outsource their products and, frankly, in most cases it's just not worth the hassle.

All of my licensed products are made outside the United States, but my licensees handle everything. I have never done it on my own, and for good reason. Here's what I've learned about trying to get your product manufactured abroad:

■ You have to commit to manufacturing huge quantities, which costs a ton of money, and the cost is usually prohibitive for an independent inventor.

■ The pile of paperwork that's necessary is roughly the height of an alp. Bigger companies have contacts and are all set up, but individual inventors don't and aren't. Interestingly, I've been hearing lately about more big companies coming back to the United States for various reasons, including the fact that foreign manufacturing sometimes ends up not being as economical as it first appears.

■ Some foreign countries make a practice of stealing intellectual properties, and the cost of protecting your product from this kind of rip-off is exorbitant.

■ The process is terribly confusing. You have to deal with a lot of potentially difficult and complicated issues from the get-go: up-front money, quality control, customs, safety regulations, and the language barrier. Basically, you'll need a crash course in everything from the document requirements for customs to product safety requirements, wire transfers from bank to bank, and what's involved for the shipment inspection agency. It's a maze.

■ You really need an agent or broker, so your product doesn't get stuck in limbo somewhere because the proper paperwork isn't ready. But that means you have to check all references and credentials and talk to their customers—and even then it's hard to be certain how reputable or competent that person or company is. Plus the agent or broker will take a chunk of your money for the services provided.

■ Quality control can be an issue with foreign manufacturers. When I tried ordering a couple of samples, the end products seemed shoddily made. If my name is on something, I want it to be perfect.

There are online companies that put you in touch with foreign suppliers, but you must do your research on these, as well as talk to people who have used them. I just don't feel comfortable with this arrangement because I don't know anyone who has used them and it seems far too risky, and there have been lots of complaints about many of them.

I realized early on that foreign manufacture wasn't consistent with my vision for my companies and products. For one thing, if you manufacture abroad, you're stuck with your original design until inventory sells out, and I'm a tweaker: I love to be able to adjust and improve my products. For example, one shipment of the mirror component I used for my in-house car seat mirror assembly once came to me with a rough edge. It was no big deal for me to sand each one smooth, but if the finished product had been packaged in another country, I would have had a problem. Similarly, when I decided I wanted a hole drilled to accommodate a rivet, it was easy to do here, but if my product had already been packaged and was coming from another country, I would have been forced to wait until I ran out of inventory before I could make the change—and that might have meant living unhappily for a long time with something I wanted to alter quickly. And a final example (if you weren't already convinced): I could keep the fabric patterns and choices for my Hat Wrap current and trendy, which I couldn't have done if it had been made in China, since shipping samples back and forth and all the resulting communication red tape take tons of time.

The Made-In-America Advantage

While you can farm out the manufacture and assembly of your product to an American company that will do it all for you (for a price), my advice to you is to order your components from American companies and assemble and package your products yourself. Aside from the obvious help-grow-the-economy appeal, if you order your components from a U.S. company, the process is streamlined and fast. Many American companies import the parts you need from foreign countries, but they've done all the work for you, the price is still reasonable, and they won't require huge minimum orders.

Of course, you can always try to find an American company that will manufacture and assemble the whole thing for you from soup to nuts, but in most cases, doing your own small run of products at home or in an inexpensive rental space is the most economical way to go, until the orders get so big that you need to grow. The big profits won't happen until you go on to bigger quantities, but at least you're not spending tons of money up front and sitting on a lot of inventory. Also, you can tweak your product easily and quickly if necessary—and chances are you'll have to.

If your product isn't something you can put together at home (like a toothbrush that has to be injection-molded, for example), you will need to find a company to manufacture the entire thing for you. All of my products have been based on my ability to get components and assemble them myself, but not every inventor has that option.

How to Assemble at Home: DIY

I've found these steps are helpful if you go the DIY route:

- If you made a prototype you will already know what components you will need. (See Chapter 11 for details.)

■ Once you know what your components are, go online to sleuth the best and least expensive ways to get them. It's super-easy now to find manufacturers: just type in whatever you need and search it, and companies pop right up. Contact companies for samples before you order. When I was researching mirrors for my car seat accessory invention, I experimented with locker and bike mirrors. Then I found a local mirror manufacturer through Thomasnet.com (a great place to find manufacturers of supplies you need for your prototypes or actual products) that I was able to visit. I told them what I needed and the company sent me a whole range of samples. Some were too thin, others distorted the image too much, but one—like Goldilocks' porridge—was just right.

■ If you run up against a part that costs a lot, think creatively. Plastic products, for instance, are usually made from a mold, and the up-front cost for making one is pretty substantial, plus the minimum order you have to place is often huge. When I needed a plastic part for the back of my mirror, I knew I didn't want to pay for a mold and I also didn't want to order thousands of pieces yet, so I looked up plastic companies in my area, visited a few, and asked a lot of questions about how I could get this done without having to make an injection mold. I found a small company in Boston that said it could cut the piece and heat-bend it to the proper angle. The per-piece rate was a little high but reasonable, and the minimums were perfect. The owner was nice and helpful too.

■ Keep in mind that technology is now favoring the independent inventor: things like 3D printers are coming down in price and are more readily available now, so you can make plastic pieces at home or in your local workshop.

■ Have fun problem solving! I can't tell you how many tries it took before

I ditched what I thought I had to have and tried something totally differ-ent that worked even better (like using a rivet instead of messy adhesive or tape for the car seat mirror). I've also been able to repurpose components I'd already purchased for one invention to use on another. For instance, I had a customized strap made for my car seat mirrors when I was still as-sembling them myself. But once it was licensed and no longer needed the straps, I could use them on the Hat Wrap.

■ Once you have your parts, start problem solving the assembly. Often you will need to invent a device or a process to make the assembly faster and easier, and geared toward efficiency and economy. When I got my first big batch of orders, I had to find a way to make a dozen car seat mirrors at a time, so I made a simple but effective device from a piece of wood I found in the basement, adding slots to drop the mirrors in and marking where each piece should go, using a black marker. It worked so well I ended up making several of them.

■ Now you need to think about packaging. An inexpensive option for smaller products is the polybag, with a sheet of typed directions inserted if necessary. You can also print a nice header and staple it to the top. Uline. com sells many sizes and thicknesses of polybags as well as devices to seal them shut, and also offers many supplies for shipping. If you want some-thing more elaborate, you'll need to get help from your graphic designer and/or a good printing company, which can be a bit costly but allows you to print a box or clamshell plastic package with eye-catching designs. If you get your product into the bigger box stores, you'll need a UPC code (a bar code) printed on your packaging. General-search "universal product code" to find out how to do it.

Resources for DIY Assembly

You may not have space in your basement or garage (or kitchen!) to assemble and package your products. Or you may have toddlers running about underfoot, so you have an instant safety (and sanity) issue on your hands. If you're sure you can't go the no-overhead route of the home shop, or if orders get too big for you to handle alone, you need to decide on an alternative. Work training centers for people with disabilities may be an excellent way to go: you can feel good about offering work to a population that often has difficulties finding it, and even though the process takes some training, it becomes a win-win for both sides. You can also revisit the ideas in Chapter 11 for renting space inexpensively.

What if you need more help or you don't have time to do all the hands-on assembly work yourself? For outside per-project help, rather than committing to hiring employees, try TaskRabbit.com or Craigslist.org. Or you could put up a flyer at your local vocational school: many students or new grads would love to practice their skills and get on-the-job experience while earning a little money.

Once you've set up your business for one product, you'll know the drill: you will now have a workable framework and you won't have to keep reinventing the wheel for any products you come up with later.

Now it's time to figure out all the bells and whistles that will seduce your customers, give your product a longer shelf life, and prolong its buying appeal. Read on!

15

Bedazzle It (Step Six)

Add Bells and Whistles

Sometimes what you think is just icing turns out to be even better than the cake.

—MAG HAWKWOOD

Once you have a real product, and it's actually selling itself online or on store shelves, you may think you can just sit back, relax, and collect your payments. But the worst thing for an inventor is complacency: you always need to be thinking ahead. And you also need to cultivate thinking big: stay open to the idea of riding the bigger wave, and your products will only improve. I'm talking at this point about adding enhancements to a product that is already selling—taking advantage of a proven winner to generate more streams of income, while sometimes keeping the original design. I'm not advocating trying to make a silk purse out of the proverbial sow's ear; you can't bedazzle something that's not selling well. But if your brainchild is a success, other inventors or companies will likely jump on the bandwagon and try to cash in on variations of your product. You might as well do it first.

Think of it this way: every product comes with a sort of built-in shelf life, and that's why we need to keep next-generation improvements and enhancements in mind. If we add some bells and whistles to an existing product, we breathe new life into it and extend that shelf life just a bit more.

How have people done it? In dozens of ways.

WHY PEOPLE BUY

It's no secret that the phrase "New and Improved" on a label is an instant buyer magnet. Why? Because people get tired of the same old, same old. We want novelty. We crave excitement and pleasure. And many, many of us are hoping to find these things when we haul out our wallets to make a purchase. Buying stuff isn't always about meeting basic needs; it also creates feelings of power and pleasure. That's why you need to be sure there's something in your product that keeps attracting people and making them want to buy it year after year.

Think about how dull things would be if everything were stripped down to just the simplest basics. Can you imagine a life of endless oatmeal with no cinnamon or raisins or dried cranberries or walnuts or whatever? As inventors, we want to be sure we add interest and zest to our products so that they're more fun, more interesting, more attractive, and more worthy of purchase so that more people will keep on wanting them.

The inventing business is filled with countless examples of enhancements and improvements. Take the lowly grocery cart, for example. When some brilliant inventor added a cup holder to the basic cart design, she or he guaranteed that shoppers could spend more time in the store (hence adding more items to their carts) as they sipped their brew. Or think of the key ring, something most of us need to keep all our various keys in one convenient place. Well, now we have tiny flashlights on key rings, or bottle openers, or nail files, or safety whistles, or thumb drives.

Many inventions are set in motion by a simple desire and then take off from there. Here's a good example: wanting to listen to a favorite song. We started with record players, then went on to 8-track recorders, then cassette recorders, CDs, and now mp3 players—an evolution that began with something basic. Whenever something "catches on" with the public, inventors like us are inspired to come up with another, better (or at least different) version of the same product. Keeping up with technology is a great motivator: we all want to be the first to cash in on something. Think of those old-style dolls that talked when you pulled a string. Toy inventors were quick to grab onto the new digital recording technology, and they revolutionized how dolls talk. Now the pull-string method is *so* last century.

Coffeemakers are another example. Now it's no longer enough to have a pot-sized drip coffeemaker; you have to get one of those fancy things with little expensive one-serving cups. Some may call them elitist, but the new technology gives personal flavor choices and the ability to personalize something, which is often what it's all about. Many cars—the Mini Cooper, for instance—can be customized to your specifications online: you just point and click at what you want and then you go pick it up, a sort of Build-A-Bear Workshop for cars. People love products that give them the capacity to be unique.

Or think about what's happened with water. There's really nothing more basic than water, but after being persuaded by savvy advertisers that we should drink fancy designer brands from bottles, now there are waters with added flavors, vitamins, and minerals.

Water-with-additions is only one of many extra-benefit inventions. Think of heated car seats, or dog treats that freshen Fido's breath. Then there's makeup with sunscreen added, or chewing gum that whitens your teeth.

It's always good to think of adding something to your product that will give it extra value. And some additions are just for fun, like the interior lights in my car that change colors, so you can create and change the "mood" in your car just for the kick of it.

Then there's the cachet or "cool" factor—which leads me to the next section.

FADS, TRENDS, AND NAME BRANDS

Fads and fashions come and go. Remember when everybody was paying top dollar to add to their Beanie Baby collection? Or, even longer ago, when Chia Pets were the rage? Or Pet Rocks? Or Lava Lamps? Or . . . you get the idea. Like skirt lengths and lipstick colors, even dog breeds go in and out of fashion. Fashion is one way for smart designers to keep making money, because the fact is that nobody will buy anything if what they have is enough. It's all about manufacturing desire.

There is a difference, though, between fads and trends. Fads are like the daily weather, changing rapidly. We can sometimes cash in on a flash-in-the-pan fad just as savvy department stores make a killing on rainy days if they put inexpensive umbrellas near the door. We need to be sure we're aware of the fads and fashions today—or be so brave that we create them ourselves. But we also need to know which way the prevailing cultural winds are blowing. A trend is like an overall weather pattern—a full winter season, for instance, as compared to the "fad" of a sudden snow squall.

A savvy inventor needs to be aware of today's trends. Take the eco-friendly, all-natural, "green" trend, for instance: If you can make your product from earth-friendly materials, you'll want to shout that fact from the rooftops—or at least announce it prominently on the packaging—because this appears to be a trend that is going to be with us for a long time. Going back to the water and coffee phenomena, adding awareness of the eco-friendly trend explains the plethora of stainless steel water bottles designed to replace those nasty plastic ones, and ceramic coffee to-go cups instead of disposables.

Then there are name brands.

While everybody likes to appear unique, people also crave "fitting in," especially young people. When a frugal friend of mine bought her kids generic snacks for lunch, her kids were made fun of at school. She caved and bought a name brand for them, even though it basically tasted the same as the less expensive kind. Even yellow No. 2 pencils have to be name brand if kids want to feel accepted in the middle school here.

Name brands have an instant-recognition factor, which can make people feel safe at the same time that it makes them feel as if they are on some cutting edge. My licensee did a brilliant bells-and-whistles addition on my car seat mirror by adding *Sesame Street* characters around the frame. Instantly there was more demand for the enhanced product, rather than the plain version.

People want the latest and greatest, so they can be perceived as cool and popular. When people talk about "creating a brand," this is partly what they mean—and I'll tell you all about how to do it yourself in Chapter 16. Each of us wants our brand to be recognizable, respected, and sought-after. We all want to be the cool new brand on the block that everybody wants.

There are three building blocks for creating enhancements for your product:

1. *Add something.* What can you add to give extra appeal, like those freeze-dried berries in cereal? Often, the addition of music, light, or sound to any product makes it more appealing. The car mirror eventually included all of those features, so those bedazzled options became moneymakers in addition to the other versions already out there. Here in Boston, smart gas stations have added TV screens to the pumps so people can be bombarded by ads while they fill up.

2. *Vary it.* Different colors, shapes, and sizes of things can keep them popular (think of the iPod line, for instance, or all the thousands of available cell phone covers). If your product includes fabric, you can change it to keep it looking fresh and contemporary. You could incorporate current fashions or fads, or seasonal varieties of things, like a green milkshake that only comes out in time for St. Patrick's Day.

3. *Think of extra uses for it.* Are there other creative ways your product might be used? For instance, my dog waste disposal kit can also be used as a traveling water bowl. If I decide to market it as that, it would mean an extra income stream that would generate more royalties.

Now that you've followed the six steps to invention, you're ready for an all-important chapter: Building the Right Online Platform for You. It will help you establish a command central from your computer or other devices, and sell like crazy all over the web for practically nothing!

16

Building the Right Online Platform

Social Media Tricks and Tools to Make Your Product Flourish

Only connect.
    —E.M. FORSTER

It just amazes me that we can sit at our computers (or pick up our tablets or smartphones or some other personal device) in our own little homes or offices—or anywhere!—and be instantly connected to millions of people. What a wonder! And the wave of potential for marketing products using online social media hasn't even begun to crest. By the time you read this, there will be a new app or network or two to help you beef up the buzz for your brainchild. But for now, think of the numbered sections in this chapter as the basic boards that will help you build the right platform to support your dreams and elevate your products so more people can see and appreciate them. Just be warned: this chapter applies to *protected ideas only*, so be sure to read Chapter 12.

People are spending more and more time on their personal devices, and doing more of their shopping and buying online—it's become our entertainment—so a little familiarity with the six points in this chapter will help any inventor join the 21st century and leave the dinosaurs in the dust.

Basically, the online world is offering you a wonderful opportunity that you don't want to miss: online buying and advertising are the way commerce is rapidly heading.

The technology can seem overwhelming, but you don't need to be afraid of it. Just remember this: you don't have to be a techie or a computer nerd to use the Internet and social media to grab people's attention. Anyone can do it. Most of it is free. It works for you 24/7. And it works like magic. But you must be patient and learn how to use it effectively, studying it and then using it to engage with people. You don't need to build Rome in a day—take it step by step at a pace that feels right for you, and concentrate on being authentic in all you do there. Your uniqueness and genuineness will help you attract the attention and audience you need.

The Internet can be totally time-consuming, so be sure you balance your time on the web with the rest of your life. While I check my feeds and e-mail constantly throughout the day, I spend only about 30 minutes every morning scheduling my posts for that day and maybe the next. If I get any comments or questions, I try to answer them within 24 hours. But if something interesting happens anytime during the day or evening, I share it on all my social media networks. It may sound like a lot to build into your day, but I've found that it's worth it. (And I've discovered some shortcuts: Even though I may be taking a risk of ruining my phone, I often do my posting and status updates while I'm in the bathtub! And some of us put timers on our computers so we don't sit at them too long.)

Sure, by now we're all familiar with the term "social media," but maybe it will be helpful for you to think of these online services the way I do—as "emotional media." Here's why: they connect us individually with others, and we're a culture starving for connection. The web is just a way of using new tools to have a one-on-one relationship with people. It also lets us provide great customer service, which has really been lost everywhere (think of all those interminable minutes spent on hold while a computer-ized voice plays over and over). Individual attention builds loyal custom-ers, and online tools show us the human face and human story behind a product; they touch our hearts. As online stories, songs, products, and posters go viral, we can see the huge capacity for the online phenomenon to affect us, change us, move us.

COMMON MISCONCEPTIONS ABOUT SOCIAL MEDIA

People who don't already use social media may not understand the wonderful possibilities it holds for you and your ideas. Here are a few of the most common misconceptions.

It's not really a business tool. Actually, social media can be one of your most valuable business tools, since it is usable for so many aspects of your busi-ness: public relations, marketing, market research, sales, customer service, and more. It also gives you the ability to find and contact almost anyone directly and quickly.

I don't have time to learn it and implement it. Oh yes you do! It's better to spend some time learning about the web rather than wasting valuable time on more traditional methods that aren't working all that well anymore. Just start building it into your day (and/or night). Always remember that these tools are free—so it makes sense to invest a little time in free marketing, free promotion, and customer outreach. Just think, if large multinational conglomerates and internationally known brands are reaching out to potential customers and current customers through social media outlets, why shouldn't you?

I don't see the potential for any big return on investment. Au contraire, the Internet gives you the tools to make connections with people all around the world that you never would have gotten otherwise—and again, for the most part, those tools are free. Keep in mind that connection is what makes loyal customers. Think referrals, sales, joint ventures. Publishers, for example, really see the value; before many will take a chance on acquiring your manuscript, they want to be sure you have a good-size online audience that you can use to promote your book. Anything you do on social media helps your name to get higher up in the rankings. For instance, I just got a call from someone in London who found me on the first page of a Google search for speakers about inventing. And that's because I've been busily "tagging" my YouTube videos (keep reading and you'll find out what that means) as well as all my other posts and other social media activity.

I've seen some Facebook posts and Twitter tweets and, frankly, I don't care if people know I had pizza for dinner. There is a much larger equation here than the minutia of your day! You're helping people get to know you, making you more transparent and authentic, so you become trustworthy, as well as more human and relatable.

BRANDING ON THE WEB

In the last chapter, I talked a little bit about "brands." The truth is that everyone is branding themselves online, whether they intend to or not, because the posts they make or the images they share are a kind of brand: their messages are being burned into the minds of their viewers. You can do it, too—with a twist! You can use the web to build a trustworthy, compelling brand that will get your product out there and onto the radar screens of millions.

Brands speak to people on an emotional or subliminal level. A good brand will offer a feeling experience to a customer. And if a brand is compelling and eye-catching enough, it becomes immediately recognizable and therefore familiar and trustworthy.

Over time I decided to brand my personal name because I had several products and services, not just one, and I wanted to gather them under a general umbrella. It would have been a pain to have a separate website, Twitter account, Facebook page, etc., for each one. Also, I am branding myself as a product developer, speaker, and consultant, so this way everything is under my name. If you are planning on having more than one invention or idea—and chances are that you will—then you may want to consider branding your company name or your personal name so you too can have a broad umbrella.

Once some of my products were licensed, the licensee produced the sites for them, so I didn't have to. Having everything under my own personal name meant that I could take products off the site when they were licensed without making it look like I'd gone out of business.

I spent a lot of time looking at different social media platforms, and I waited to do my own until I had an idea of the image, or brand, that I wanted to present. I paid particular attention to popular people with interesting posts and a lot of followers. And I found out something really interesting: they were not hard-selling at all. They were just constantly sharing fun and informative information. I realized how important it is to stay relevant and generous: when a post offered some kind of value for me, I just naturally wanted to click on the author's profile and website to learn more about that person. I felt connected to her or him after just a few online visits. Sometimes I would enter my e-mail address on the person's website so I could receive newsletters or other services, which is exactly what the site's owner was hoping I'd do. Collecting e-mail addresses without making it screamingly obvious that you're doing so is one of the most important intentions you can have online, because doing that will give you a ready-made list of possible customers. Think about it: people are constantly checking their e-mail, so e-mail marketing can be effective as long as it's not mass e-mail blasting, which, it could be argued, falls under the category of annoyance. And which usually ends up in our spam folders anyway.

The Internet gives business a human face. Thanks to the web, you can listen to people and offer solutions to their problems, target your audience perfectly, build membership for your goods and services, and grow your business, all at the same time. If the content on your posts offers value to people, they'll share it with others, comment on it, or "like" it, which will place you higher in the rankings, which means your name may start popping up when people search for certain terms, which means more people will see your stuff and share it—and on and on, in a positive kind of snowball effect. Basically, if you offer interesting or informative material online, you'll develop a following and eventually gain a reputation as a trustworthy and honest expert—which you can turn into profits down the line.

Let's look at how *you* can begin to harness the power of the Internet to inspire others and connect with the world.

1. WEAVING A WEBSITE

If you have a product to sell, you need a website. In the old days, people handed out business cards and brochures. Now we also give people our web address. This is the only one of my six points that will cost you money, since you'll need to pay for a domain name and hosting even if you build the website yourself, the way I did. But it's a must, and it's worth it.

How to Purchase a Domain Name

Go to networksolutions.com or godaddy.com and type in the name you want to use to be sure somebody else hasn't grabbed it. Remember that you will get one domain name free with your website. Any additional domain names can be bought for a minimum of a year, and you only have to buy a dot-com, not a dot-net or a dot-org. Start simple. I recommend that you start out by buying your own name for your primary website (for instance, my web address is PatriciaNolanBrown.com). You can also buy a domain name for each of your products (like my ParachuteDog.com) that will send people back to your main website.

Why do you need a website? There are three big reasons:

1. These days if you don't have a website, it's as though you don't exist. Customers and store buyers need to have a place they can go to learn who you are and what your products are all about.

2. You need a place that will be the hub for all your online activity, including selling products, or telling people where to buy them, and a way to collect customer e-mail addresses.

3. Most customers will be looking for you and your products online, through search engines, so they need to be able to search for and find you ahead of others offering similar products, which means that your website needs search engine optimization (SEO). One component of SEO is keywords (see sidebar).

What Are SEO Keywords?

They're words that people will naturally use when they are searching for a specific product on an online search engine. If you use these words on your website, this will help your product to show up higher on the result page of their searches. When I invented a cleaner, quicker way to pick up and dispose of dog poop, I made sure the phrase "dog waste bags" was all over my website where it was relevant, so my website would show up when people searched for a product to scoop Fluffy's poop.

For help choosing keywords or phrases, do a general search for free keyword tools. Once you get to the tool, type in your idea and you'll see how many people actually type that word into a search.

If you're curious about the keywords your competition is using, go to a competitor's website, click on your browser's View button, and choose either "View Source" or "Page Info," which will give you the site's HTML (hypertext markup language) code, listing the keywords separated by commas.

In general, a *good* website has:

➤ A way to identify you and/or your product immediately and grab the reader.

➤ User-friendly design, so anyone can navigate it. Be sure it's interesting without being overly busy or complicated—no clutter! The look and feel of your website experience is what equals your brand.

➤ Search engine optimization keywords.

➤ Photos or other visuals to give people information about you and your products.

➤ Your main information and opt-in box located above the fold line, since 80 percent of viewers never scroll down. And since that's so, use tabs to help readers get around your site, rather than using long pages.

➤ A "Like" button and a "Share" button so people can indicate their approval of each page of your website, and easily share it with their friends.

➤ Icons that link to your social media networks, above the fold and in the top right. (I'll be walking you through all the different social media later in this chapter.)

What Is an Opt-In Box?

It's a short form where readers can enter their e-mail addresses for you to keep in exchange for sending out a newsletter or download or whatever. Think of it as a nice live trap for capturing e-mail addresses so you can send e-mail marketing to your site visitors.

➤ A contact form so that people can get in touch with you (and people seem to prefer a form rather than just an e-mail address).

➤ Something you give free of charge to everyone who visits your site: an inspiring quote, or a download of a how-to article, or a bargain or goodie in exchange for readers' e-mail addresses (this is the use of the opt-in box). You can use the collected addresses for setting up future advertising.

➤ A version that looks good on a mobile phone screen. Mobile is huge, since phones go with you everywhere, and most website hosts have a mobile version you can simply click to activate.

What's a "Fold"?

Whatever you see on your screen when you arrive at a site is "above the fold." If you have to scroll down, you've gone below it. This came from the days when people folded their newspapers in half to read them.

A *great* website has all that a good one does as well as:

➤ Juicy and compelling text.

➤ A "storefront" page for ordering your products online. Check this out with your web host: you can eliminate stores and sell to consumers directly so you can keep all the profits for yourself.

➤ Visuals that are not only informative, but expressive, attractive, and memorable.

➤ Super-short demo video(s).

➤ An FAQ tab—FAQ stands for "Frequently Asked Questions"—that a customer can click on for quick answers without having to go through the whole website.

➤ Going to a great website is like walking into a store—a Starbucks, for instance. It uses striking graphics, colors, and other elements to shape how people perceive you. It becomes an emotional experience. That's what builds your "brand"—and it's very important.

What about a Logo?

It's best to have one, since a logo looks professional and helps give readers a shorthand way to remember you and your product. If you do have one, it can be used as your photo in all your social media. If you don't have a logo yet, don't worry: just use your name or your product name to begin building your brand recognition.

Spend some time surfing the web to find the sites that grab your attention and keep it. Notice what they have in common, and what sets them apart. Start thinking about the words you want to use to describe your product. What benefits does it offer? People want to know what's in it for them. Use photos. Maybe even do a short video for the site, using it to demonstrate your product in action—people love to watch moving objects! Just keep your video under one minute, and keep in mind that the most valuable video is one that shows how your product works. You can use your phone along with a cool app, such as Vine or Instagram, which gives you the ability to make short videos, upload them to YouTube, and embed them on your website. There are plenty of other helpful apps as well.

There are a lot of web design experts out there making major ducats, and for good reason: it can be tricky to come up with the perfect recipe for a great website. But if you're on a budget, you can try using a website-building tool yourself. If you go the DIY route, I recommend Network Solutions (networksolutions.com), which is very user-friendly and has great customer service. It keeps up with all the latest features and options, like creating surveys and polls so you can actually tweak your product to make it more appealing to potential buyers, based on the results.

A Word about the Numbers

Although there are services that offer users the ability to purchase page views, likes, and fans, doing so is viewed as fraudulent and unethical by most users of social media sites—and in turn, if you've bought likes, fans, or page views, you and your brilliant new product may be viewed as equally fraudulent. Admittedly, it takes a little time to build a following organically, but by doing the right things and respecting the informal and unwritten rules of each social media outlet, you actually build a great deal of respect (which helps build an even greater following).

It's good for information on you or your product to appear higher up on a search results page, but don't drive yourself crazy over it. You can pay extra through website companies—or any marketing company—to get your name rankings higher in a search, but there's no guarantee it will work, and there's another way to do it that's free: generate lots of links between your website and your blog, Facebook posts, Twitter tweets, and anything you do online (keep reading!). Think of it as a spider's web: it's all in the connections between the threads.

Just keep in mind that you can build your website yourself with easy-to-use tools and templates provided by your web host company, which will also offer you 24/7 free help—at least, Network Solutions does. Take as long as you need to build it: the public won't see it until you're ready and you hit the Publish button. Another advantage to doing the site yourself is that you can edit it anytime—you're in total control. So jump in and experiment! I guarantee that you will impress yourself.

The Goals for Your Website

➤ Maximize your search engine optimization keywords and phrases.

➤ Keep your content up-to-date.

➤ Choose a domain name that expresses what you do or describes the product you want to promote.

➤ Make it easy for people to find you and your products by promoting your web address on everything you send out, whether printed or digital.

➤ Offer something of value to readers so you can get their e-mail addresses with your opt-in box.

➤ Create a memorable brand for yourself.

➤ Test your goods online with polls on your website so you can get valuable feedback from potential customers.

➤ Sell your goods online.

If you weave it well, your website will catch a lot of positive attention for you.

2. TO BLOG OR NOT TO BLOG

Some pundits say that long, wordy blogging is going out of fashion because there are just too many blogs on the web, but crafting a short, visual, snappy, unique blog can be a great way to establish a connection with people who may be interested in you and your product.

First, choose your preferred medium:

➤ A mostly written blog with stories (probably not the best way for an inventor to go)

➤ A photo blog with captions

➤ A video blog

Creating a compelling blog was definitely on my to-do list. But I wanted to be a little different, and since I tend to be a visual learner myself, I decided to make a video blog. If you like showing rather than telling, that might be the route for you, too, or you can include lots of interesting photos and keep text to a minimum. We are a visual culture, and people love looking at pictures. Check out Instagram, a free photo and video app that allows you to share your photos and videos with all of your social media contacts.

There are many blogsites that offer a variety of easy-to-use templates and free hosting (WordPress, Tumblr, or Blogger.com, for instance), so you can get started quickly. Sites like WordPress, Tumblr, Blogger, and others also allow users to link their blogs to their personal Facebook pages, their Facebook fan pages, and their Twitter accounts through a couple of clicks and some simple forms. Whenever you post anything on your blog, these blog services automatically send to those sites—often with a little teaser. It actually does lead to more interest to your blog and more page hits.

The Goals for Your Blog

➤ Generate regular and fresh content and link to your website to raise your search rankings. If you don't have any fresh ideas, it's okay to quote content from another source as long as you credit the author.

➤ Bring new readers to you and your products.

➤ Ask readers to "like" or "share" your content if they like it and include buttons so they can do it easily. This will expand your readership.

➤ After searching the web to find similar blogs, comment on them or list them on your own site as helpful or favorite blog sites, so that yours may get referenced on their "favorites" lists.

➤ Share useful or valuable information with others.

➤ Get people to subscribe to your blog.

➤ Get enough visitors to your blog to capture the interest of advertisers that will actually offer you money to place their ads on your blog.

➤ Include a "resource box" at the end of your blog, using a maximum of three hyperlinks that will connect people back to your website.

➤ Join free blog-distributing sites like www.squidoo.com or www.hubpages.com. When you submit your blog articles to them, search engines will grab them!

Also, many hosting sites are affiliated with blog sites, so you can access a blog template in the same place. If you get enough viewer attention (by cross-promoting it everywhere online), you may even be approached by advertisers who will give you money for the privilege of placing an ad on your blog. That way, you get paid to promote your work. That's not a bad deal.

What's a Hyperlink?

Hyperlinks are words or phrases, underlined and usually in blue, that will send you directly to another site when a reader clicks on it. If you're using a link to send people to your own website, it's called a backlink. For example, on my YouTube video blog I include a sentence with three backlinks: "Patricia Nolan-Brown is an inventor, speaker, and consultant who shares free inventor tips." Clicking on my name or on the words "inventor, speaker, consultant" and "free inventor tips" will send readers directly to my website. I use this to help raise my rankings.

Blogs are a great creative outlet, and they spread the word about you and your fantastic ideas while keeping your name in the public eye. Click the Blog tab to check out my video blog at patricianolanbrown.com.

3. MAKING FRIENDS WITH FACEBOOK

No wonder so many of us are on Facebook. It helps us to stay in touch with friends and family. It reminds us of birthdays and events. It offers lots of amusing, irritating, and inspiring ways to waste time. And it can also help you spread the word about your product. People trust things that come to them through the recommendation of friends. That's why Facebook is your new best friend.

You're only allowed to have 5,000 friends, though, and over time we all aim far higher than that, so the first thing you have to do is create a fan page for your company or products, since fan pages can have an unlimited number of subscribers. Then e-mail everybody on all your lists announcing the page and asking them to subscribe and "like" it. Fan pages can "go viral" and spread your message far and wide, because when someone subscribes to your page, all of their contacts are automatically connected to it. This way you have the potential to be linked instantly to hundreds of thousands of people. It's an easy way to let everybody know about all the latest ideas that proceed from your fertile brain! Once I created my fan page, it gave me the perfect place to share my goings-on, with photos of recent inventors' conventions, interviews, and the latest videos from my blog. People like to see what I've been up to, and Facebook is the fastest way to let them know.

You can offer product coupons, discount codes, contests, and other rewards for followers of your Facebook page. And be sure to do a lot of posts on weekends, when traffic to the site is high.

The Goals for Your Facebook Pages

➤ Create pages for yourself and your product to build interest, share valuable information, and let people know what you're doing.

➤ Post frequently and keep it relevant.

➤ Use photos—people love to look at images.

➤ Choose an appropriate cover photo for your business page. This can be a logo or a photo of your product. You don't want to feature a photo of your dog if you're trying to sell your new coffeemaker!

➤ Add friends and comment on others' posts as much as you can.

➤ Offer exclusive only-on-Facebook things once in a while.

➤ Ask open-ended questions to get people to engage and comment.

➤ Be sure to include an easy-to-find link to your website on your Facebook page.

Just remember, you can never have too many friends.

4. YOUTUBE

YouTube is a great place to upload and edit videos at no cost—and videos are hugely popular with the TV generation. You don't need to invest in expensive equipment, either; just use the video feature on your phone along with any of the fun apps that are coming out. You can create your own YouTube channel, which, like a popular blog, can attract paid advertisers and subscribers. There are even companies like Amazon Mechanical Turk (www.mturk.com) that will transcribe your video so you can post it as a written blog, which will be more easily discovered by the search engines.

Once you make a video and upload it on YouTube, you can share it with anyone who wants to see your product, or upload it privately to only share with people who have signed an NDA. Let's say you have a list of companies that are taking new product submissions. All you have to do is send them the link to your video online. How easy and fast is that?

*H*ere's a great example of someone who turned a daily video blog into a huge business: Gary Vaynerchuk, whose videos for Wine Library TV made him a celebrity. He has a lot of videos on YouTube, but you should check out one in particular, dealing with how to build a personal brand on the Internet (warning: he uses adult language). Go to YouTube and search his keynote speech at Inc 500 Seminar 2011 to hear his advice for building your own brand and how valuable social media is for promoting and selling your products.

How-to demonstrations that are less than one minute long are the way to go if you have a product you want to promote. Keep the mood light and have fun with it!

The Goals for YouTube

➤ Create fun, informative videos so people can see what your product is, how it works, and what it offers.

➤ Fill out as much information as possible for each video. One thing you will be asked to do is "tag" your video. Be sure to do this, using many appropriate search words and phrases.

➤ Under "description," put your website first, and be sure to use *http://www*, not just *www*. This will help you get the proper ranking.

➤ Embed your videos in your website and your blog. This can be done by copying the unique embed code that YouTube provides through a couple of simple clicks.

➤ Link your videos to promote your products. Include them in anything, digital or printed, that you send out, and in all of your social networks.

➤ Use video sharing sites like *www.tubemogul.com*, especially if you're doing a video blog, to get it distributed to dozens of other sites simultaneously.

➤ You can use online video-sharing apps like Vine or Instagram to make short videos that you can then upload to YouTube.

Didn't you always want to play movie director? My dad had a Super-8 camera for home movies of our family ski trips and other events, and I had a childhood passion for Gumby, so my friend and I used Dad's camera to make our own claymation videos. It was some of the best times I've ever spent. It can be fun to create your own show, and this is such a painless way for people to learn about you and your products and ideas.

5. TWEETS: SHORT AND SWEET

Shakespeare was right when he said, "Brevity is the soul of wit," and the proof is the surging popularity of Twitter. Who knew so many people could be so brilliantly clever in just 140 characters? Tweeting on Twitter is perfect for all of us with limited attention spans. Besides, as stretched for time as we are, who wants to waste precious minutes on tedium? Twitter is like candy: it's fun and a little addictive, and it is the magic business tool that leads people back to your website or blog. But you do have to keep two rules in mind:

1. Keep it streamlined and clever: 140 characters can be funny and direct, with no filler.

2. Most important, even if you have a product you want to Tweet about, *no obvious sales pitches*. Nobody likes shark-like self-promotion, especially on Twitter. Remember, it's not about high-pressure salesmanship, it's all about heart and connection, so make your tweets fun to read, educational, unique, and eye-catching. You are giving people short bytes, and the ability to click on a link to learn more if they want to.

Even though I love selling my Parachute Dog product, I would never say "Buy my dog-poop scoop!" But I might send a teaser tweet that would send people to the funny story on my blog about the time a grocery-store plastic bag we were using to scoop Coconut's waste split at the seams, leaving my husband juggling her leash, the bag, and the poop that was now falling on his shoes. (At the time I thought, "Somebody ought to invent a better way to do this." And eventually I did.) So I used Twitter to get readers to my blog and website.

You can share the links or URLs of interesting articles in a tweet—and there's a lot of really fascinating stuff on the Internet to tweet about. Of course, make sure you provide some kind of comment before the link because just posting a link without any comment is not only rude on Twitter, it can also have other users view your account as being a spam account— or think that your account has been hacked. (Usually in the case of a hacked account or a spam account, the URL in question leads to a site that sends out viruses or hacks into other accounts.)

I recently found a story on StumbleUpon, for instance, about a Japanese dog poop lottery, which ties in with Parachute Dog in a very pungent way! I've also been keeping tabs on the recent social media push about dog poop being declared dangerous, and stressing the importance of cleaning up after your pet so the waste doesn't get in the groundwater, so that's on my agenda. So is the recent craze for dog walkathons. But for the most part, I try to keep my tweets totally unrelated, keeping in mind that tweets should be informative, inspiring, and clever, but never obnoxious.

Some people only use Twitter for real-time customer support; it's an instant, quick-and-easy way to solve problems and satisfy customers. You can also see what other people are saying about both you and your competition. The way I would do this, for instance, is to type in PatriciaNolan-Brown in the "search" bar on Twitter. Then I can instantly see anything anyone has said about me or my products. Then I can type in the name of my competitors and do the same thing. This is a great way to monitor the chatter, and to engage in it.

What's a Hashtag?

A "hashtag" is the symbol # (pound sign) used before a word or phrase in a tweet. It's a link that gives people the ability to search for tweets with a common topic. For example, I often use "#dog" in my tweets, which means that anyone in the world who has also used the #dog in a tweet is now in a specific community that is talking about dogs. Bingo—my target audience. Hashtags enable us to follow threads of common interest and jump in on any conversation. They also help us in other ways. For example, if you want your product to be featured in *O Magazine*, you could do a "#Oprah" hashtag in or after your tweet in hopes that her people may notice you, because they are probably monitoring what is being said about them. Or you could hashtag a store that you think would be ideal to carry your product. Hashtags are also on other networks such as Facebook, Vine, and Instagram. Hashtags expand your community and get you and your product recognized.

What we aim for is to be "retweeted"—when someone likes your tweet so much that they send it to all their followers. It's an awesome endorsement when someone does, and increases your exposure exponentially. Keep in mind that the most common retweets are inspirational quotes.

Guy Kawasaki is a great example of a proficient Tweeter (@guykawasaki). He shares fascinating articles—how to make a better cup of coffee, for instance—and often uses eye-catching infographics. His blog posts on how to do a successful tweet are super-informative!

If your tweets are fun to read, you'll gain a following because everybody wants more fun. And if you gain a following, you'll increase your chances of building customer base and loyalty, at the same time that you create more good feeling and friendship. All in 140 characters or less.

The Goals for Twitter

➤ To get followers. You need to engage with other tweeters and "follow" them. In return they may "follow" you—or even "favorite" you, which means you'll be on their separate list of favorite tweets, and they will automatically get your tweets whenever you do one.

➤ Come up with frequent, clever, fun tweets to get more recognition for you and your message—but no overt sales pitches, please. You can include a link to your website on some of your tweets.

➤ Pique readers' interest so they will check out your Twitter profile to see what you actually do. What you want is for readers to come to your website and become customers.

➤ Make sure your website is a link on your profile so people can easily click to it.

➤ Get "retweeted"—which means people sharing your tweets with all their followers—so your name gains real clout and you get more readers and followers.

➤ Build a reputation as a credible or informative source. People will begin to look forward to your tweets and will follow you to get them.

> ➤ Use hashtags to attract attention and become part of a stream—
> just be sure not to use more than two or three hashtags per
> tweet.
>
> ➤ Use #Discover to find tweets about breaking news and what's hot
> and trending. You might get a great invention idea from some of
> them.

6. LINKING TO LINKEDIN

LinkedIn was the creation of a team of innovative thinkers who wanted an online way to forge professional connections—a sort of business equivalent of the friend-and-family-based Facebook. It has hundreds of millions of members all over the world, and it's a great way to maximize your human resources. You can use it to find the people you need in a hurry, because it's where business professionals live. Also, you can use the site to gather useful information about professional contacts, such as their education, professional interests, membership in professional groups, mutual interests, mutual connections, and more. In addition, it's a great way to find out whether connections have friends in common with you, since people would always rather do business with friends of friends.

In the bad old days, the buyers I wanted to reach were fiercely guarded by gatekeepers (administrative assistants and such) who might or might not let me speak to them. And if I did manage to get through to them, I had to travel to have a meeting—and that cost money. Now I can use LinkedIn to go right to a current and up-to-date list of buyers and find out how to contact them. Rather than traveling to meet, I can do it online, all at no cost. If you have a store in mind, for instance, you search that store on

LinkedIn by typing in the store name and the word "buyer" in the search box. A list of buyers will come up. Find the one in your category (I would search a specific pet store, for instance, and focus on the name that comes up under pet waste management—there really is such a category). If you have the buyer's full name you can search online to find contact information through her or his company website, personal Facebook pages, or any articles written about that person. If you don't get a full name—some listings are only a first name and a last initial—you could contact the specific store and ask for the person in that department by the first name. If you're searching for a licensee, the process is the same, except that you'll be typing in "category searches" (rather than store names) followed by the word "licensee" instead of "buyer." LinkedIn is also a great place to ask for and display professional recommendations and testimonials as well as personal endorsements.

The Goals for LinkedIn

➤ Set up your own LinkedIn page. If you're seeking a licensee or store buyers, you can say that on your page.

➤ Build your connections.

➤ Find targeted buyers, licensees, and customers for your products.

➤ Become part of a like-minded online community.

➤ Join many professional groups with invaluable contacts—at no cost.

➤ Get endorsements from experts in your field and list testimonials from satisfied customers about you and your products.

LinkedIn is like an international chamber of commerce that connects you to all the professionals you need. At no charge.

ADVERTISING ON THE WEB

The Internet has changed the face of marketing forever. Now you have the potential to be followed by advertisers who collect data from your online activity to see what you like and what your buying and searching patterns are. While some folks feel spied on or violated by this, I like to think of it as having a personal shopper: yay, somebody knows what I like! I'd rather that than have someone calling me in the middle of dinner or knocking on my door trying to sell me something in which I have absolutely no interest.

The hard-sell days are over, and I think that's good news. You don't need to be pushy anymore. With the Internet, you can pull people in by engaging with them and caring about them. Then they'll naturally become customers (if and when they need your product) and/or they'll recommend you to someone they know.

It is possible to buy relatively inexpensive and effective ads for your products on Facebook. And the beauty of it is that it's very targeted. For instance, I could buy an ad that would be targeted to appear on the pages of dog owners. Facebook does all the research for you. You also can buy ads on Twitter and LinkedIn.

You might also want to explore affiliate advertising programs (just general-search the phrase). The process is simple. You put a link on your site that takes the visitor to a site that sells related products. If someone clicks through and buys the product on the related site, you get a commission,

which varies depending on the program. Web hosting sites such as Go-Daddy.com and others offer this.

Another helpful tool is the ability to host an online seminar or "webinar" to share your story or expertise and create an audience for your product. Check out GoToWebinar.com and/or Spreecast.com to learn how this is done. If you set up a webinar, be sure to promote it on every social media network at your disposal.

You should also use the e-mail address list that you capture from your website opt-in box to set up automatically scheduled e-mail ads or offers through sites like iContact.com or ConstantContact.com. The cost for this is relatively low.

MANAGING YOUR ONLINE PRESENCE

Now that you have a website, a Facebook page, a blog, and a YouTube channel, and now that you're on Twitter and LinkedIn, make sure every e-mail and piece of print material you send out includes your web address, and maybe your Facebook and Twitter links. And be sure to cross-promote: when you post in one place, include the addresses for the others, so the connections can go on and on. As you figure out the best way to integrate your connections for your business, remember that you have an important and unique part to play in the web of relationship.

I've found the free website HootSuite to be super-helpful when it comes to managing all these different social media networks. If I had to upload or enter posts on every single one of them it could easily drive me nuts, but HootSuite manages everything for me.

This chapter has given you a good place to start on the web, but there are other places you might want to be online, depending on your product and your audience. Google+ and Pinterest are two possibilities, but you should also visit any other place your potential customers might be hanging out.

Now you're ready to get time- and sanity-saving tips that will help you lead the happiest and healthiest inventor's life that you possibly can.

Living the Inventor's Life

Helpful Hints for a Healthy, Happy Inventing Experience

Happiness lies in the joy of achievement and the thrill of creative effort.

—FRANKLIN D. ROOSEVELT

Think of this chapter as a cornucopia of tips for being the best—and happiest—inventor you can be. These time-tested and personally approved methods of getting the most out of your inventing life will help you keep your sanity in the midst of the inventing mayhem. If you're feeling frazzled, they will restore you to balance. And if you try some of them *before* you hit burnout, so much the better: they will prevent that awful feeling of "OMG, I can't do this!" or "There isn't enough time in the day!"

INVENT YOUR LIFE

Always remember that the principles in this book work just as well for inventing a life as they do for inventing a product!

When I think about my marriage and my family, for example, it dawned on me: I've needed all six success traits to grow it and make it work—at least so far!

Inquisitive. I was curious about this kid I met in the seventh grade. Tom was interesting and he made me laugh—and it didn't hurt that he was very, very cute. All through the years, I kept my eye on him, but I didn't think I was in his league.

Nerve. Then came prom season. My best friend and I dared each other to try to get dates—and I decided I'd make a call to Tom, my very first cold call. I even did a practice call to another guy, knowing that he already had a date.

Voice. My heart was pounding, but I did it—I found my voice—and I was shocked (and thrilled) when Tom accepted. We dated other people through college, but we always came back together, and eventually we married and had three daughters.

Energy. Really, it was my daughters who sparked my inventions and businesses. And the energy it takes to keep the family and all my business interests buzzing happily along actually feeds my energy!

Nourish. As anybody who has been in a partnership knows, it takes a lot of care to make a happy one. Add children to the mix, and you're at a whole new level!

Tenacity. Most successful relationships are composed of two people who aren't quitters, who have what it takes to hang in there when things get rocky and work to smooth them out.

What if I had never taken the chance, had never called Tom? Looking back, I can see that it wasn't only the six success traits that have been invaluable to me. The six steps to invention have been, too; I've used them to invent my own life. I thought it, cooked it, protected it, pitched it, made it, and continue to bedazzle it. So there really is something to this process.

JUST *DO* IT

If something intrigues you or calls you to take action, do it! Stop worrying about failing. So what if you fail? At least you won't go to your grave wondering what would have happened if you had tried. Some investors won't even give money to an entrepreneur unless that person has failed at least once, proving her or his resilience.

STOP OVER-THINKING

If you sit around thinking about doing something too long, you may lose out on a great opportunity. Do your prep work (if you need to), take a deep breath, and then just go for it. Remember that the "first inventor to file" law and/or the "first to market" principle (whoever gets the product to the store first) mean that the early bird will always catch the worm, so stop putting things off and get going.

THE LAW OF ATTRACTION WORKS

If you have an open mind and a good positive imagination, you will be amazed at the interesting things you'll attract into your life. I know it's become a kind of New Age maxim, but the law of attraction really does work. I'm proof. You wouldn't believe all the cool things that "just happen" to me because I try to stay open and positive.

REFRAME YOUR LANGUAGE

If you keep telling yourself "I can't," it will become a self-fulfilling prophecy. Tell yourself you *can.* The truth is that all of us have the ability to change our attitudes and go for the gold, even those who have always thought of themselves as too old or poor or dumb—or whatever—to try.

THINK YOUNG

Taken as a group, I think inventors tend to have a sense of curiosity and wonder that most of us associate with childhood. If you decide to go whole-hog and channel your inner kid, you'll have a lot more fun in life and you may come up with some great, playful ideas.

BE WEIRD

Most of the world's most successful and creative people were called "weird" or even "crazy" at some point in their lives. If someone calls you this, consider it a compliment, and say "thank you." Weird people change the world.

YOUR MOST IMPORTANT MANTRA

Joie de vivre. It's French for "joy of life" and it basically means that life can be a blast if you enjoy what you're doing and do what you enjoy. Repeat this mantra often, it will remind you to stop what you're doing if you loathe it and go do something fun for half an hour—or for a lifetime.

RELY ON THE KINDNESS OF STRANGERS

What you'll find as you continue the process of being an inventor is that most people are good, and they want to be helpful—and they get excited to meet a real, live inventor. You never want to take advantage of others' good nature, but it wouldn't hurt to relax a little and trust that most folks are basically kind. (That is, relax and trust folks as long as your ideas are protected.) For instance, I went into my local dry cleaner and asked if there was an extra piece of cardboard to experiment with, since I loved the way the dry cleaner folded shirts over the cardboard pieces I'd seen. The owner gave me a couple to play with and then ended up giving me boxes of hundreds! And she wouldn't take any payment, either. It turned out to be the perfect size and shape for packaging my Hat Wrap, and I was able to order more from the manufacturer when I needed them.

REMEMBER: THIS IS A GOOD TIME

We're very lucky to be living in an age and in a country where we are supported in our dreams. The backbone of our country is built on all these little businesses. We have such opportunity here and now. Take advantage of it. There is never a better time to be an inventor.

BE A CLEVER SQUIRREL

Be sure to save a few nuts for your retirement. You may think that time will never arrive, but believe me, it does, and it's nice to have some savings to fall back on.

EXPERT, SCHMEXPERT

Don't be intimidated by somebody's "expert" opinion. It's just an opinion—or their interpretation of what's true. *Not one* of my hired professionals has been 100 percent correct. Your own gut instincts are often more valuable—and reliable—than the "smartest" pro.

KEEP PERSPECTIVE

Remember, this is just business. The world will not cease to turn if you experience the odd failure or two. Just pick yourself up, dust yourself off, and try something else.

BE PROUD OF YOURSELF!

There really is nothing cooler than walking around the mall and seeing a giant window sign with your product on it. If it could happen for me, it could for you, too.

NUMBERS *CAN* LIE

Paying too much attention to statistics can really inhibit you. Remember that you can make your own luck and your own statistics. You can be the one who beats the odds.

THE JOYS OF HAVING YOUR OWN COMPANY

You can work in your pj's if you want to—or dress to the nines if you feel like it. You don't have to commute. You don't have a boss. You don't have to deal with backbiting or office politics. You don't have to put your kids in day care. You can take coffee breaks whenever you want to. You can set your own schedule. (It's funny how I work harder and for more hours than most 40-hour-a-week office workers, but I love it so much that it doesn't seem like a hardship. Plus nothing motivates us like knowing we're working for ourselves, not to make some Fat Cat fatter.) There is nothing as gratifying as being in charge of your own time and your own life. And your loved ones would rather hear your excitement at doing what you love instead of moaning about your lousy workday and your crazy boss. Plus you can even involve your significant others in some aspects of your work.

SURF THE WAVES

The inventor's life is filled with ups and downs, from the euphoria of a sale to the disappointment of a loss. Learn to ride those ups and downs without letting them capsize you. The secret is to keep your knees flexed and your disposition positive.

GIVE ME A "P"

Why? Because there is absolutely no substitute for *passion*. It's what starts our engines and keeps them running.

WHAT IS YOUR GIFT TO THE WORLD?

This book, along with my inventions, is my gift to you. I want my children and you, my readers, to remember that you can create your own life and follow your dream. What do you want *your* legacy to be? How do you want to be remembered?

INTERACT

An inventor's life is enriched by human interaction: you don't want to be a wild-haired geek in an ivory tower shunning all contact. Isolation is unhealthy (which is why I love trade shows, speaking engagements, and consulting so much: they're such a great excuse for a little healthy socializing). You owe it to yourself to get out there and interact with people.

EXERCISE

Sitting at a desk all day is not good for your health. Drag yourself to a gym in the morning after a couple cups of coffee, or after you do your school drop-offs (if you do them). You may find that a half-hour on the treadmill or on the elliptical, listening to music or just zoning out, will clear your head. You could also try using an exercise ball instead of an office chair, or working at a treadmill or standing desk. I sometimes work standing up at my piano (which nobody plays anymore) with my papers spread out all around me.

REFRAME FRUSTRATION

If there are no licensees in sight, turn the frustration into fuel for creating a great business on your own.

BUILD IN TAMIKA TIME

"Tamika Time" is a catchphrase in my family. Once, my daughter Taylor and I were on our way to a speaking engagement (I was the speaker) with very little time to spare and we decided to go to a nearby store for a quick snack. Our checkout clerk was named Tamika and, bless her heart, she was very, very slow, and didn't know how to ring up Taylor's coupons correctly (Taylor was a college kid on a budget). A manager was called. They argued. Time was ticking by and my hair was turning grayer by the moment. Finally Tamika figured it out, but we had to *sprint* to the event. The moral of the story is always, *always* build in Tamika Time for your appointments. Why? Because sh*t happens. That is the way life is.

CULTIVATE TRUST

As long as you're doing your work, there is a Tao-like wisdom in letting go and trusting that things will work out as they are meant to. When you meet life with an attitude of open curiosity and a kind of "Gosh, I wonder what *this* will teach me?" attitude, you can't go wrong. You may find, as I have, that serendipity will start to occur with greater and greater frequency.

When you decide you don't have to play god and control every little thing—when you allow things to unfold—it sure makes life less stressful. And it creates space for the Great Imagination (which I can guarantee is more imaginative than you or I) to come up with a fascinating solution or two.

BE CAREFUL

You do not have to sell the farm in order to make your inventing dreams come true. Keep a sense of perspective. It's all too easy to have tunnel vision about your idea and gamble on it, risking everything. Protect yourself.

WRITE IT OFF

You'd be amazed at the things you can use as tax deductions if you're an inventor. Check with your accountant to see what can be legitimately written off.

DAMN THE TORPEDOES! FULL SPEED AHEAD

Don't let the fact that you have no experience stop you. Everyone had to start someplace, and so do you. If you're surrounded by naysayers, plug your ears. What do they know?

TURN YOUR FEAR INTO YOUR CAREER

It's been said that Thomas Edison invented the light bulb because he was afraid of the dark. I was afraid something was wrong with my baby daughter and I couldn't see her—and that's why I invented the car seat mirror. Fears can be great motivators to find solutions.

WHEN YOU HIT AN OBSTACLE

Leave it alone for a while and then come back to it. You will probably figure it out.

WHEN THE OBSTACLE REFUSES TO BUDGE

Try it one more time and if that doesn't do it, smile and move on.

THE IMPORTANCE OF ETHICS

If you don't have integrity, you will feel lousy about yourself. Always behave in an ethical way so you can feel good about yourself and build a reputation as someone who can be trusted.

KEEP YOUR MIND FLEXIBLE

Nothing promotes creativity like a little stimulation:

➤ Sometimes I go to the library and randomly pull a magazine or book off the shelf and flip through it. The things I read or see will get my brain working and thinking. And I find that the tactile experience is feeding me, too.

➤ I love to go to stores and study the products featured on the end caps—just for fun.

➤ I get a huge kick out of noticing little mundane details. For instance, did you ever really look at the door handles on restaurants and hotels? Check out the handles on the doors at Chili's. They're works of art—and a great example of branding, since that company is giving you an experience everywhere you look.

➤ Go to a LinkedIn group and see who is "talking."

➤ Stare out your window and let your mind wander. Or focus on tree bark or leaves.

➤ Sometimes ritual or prayer can get your mind into a space that lets in ideas.

➤ Be curious about the way things are made. Look at the shoes or purse you are wearing. How are they constructed? Figuring out how things are put together can be very mind-expanding.

➤ Get out of your routine for a few days. Shut off the TV, computer, and cell phone and see what happens to your thoughts.

BE YOURSELF

You are not your parents or siblings or kids. You are *you*, a one-of-a-kind unique person with amazing ideas and thoughts and dreams. You don't have to impress anybody but yourself. You have your own kind of intelligence. So start right now this minute to believe in yourself. *Do* it yourself. Refuse to be intimidated. Be stubborn. Feed your dreams. Nobody can really predict what will sell and what won't. There is no reason why your product might not make a million dollars. But what matters most of all is that you're enjoying being yourself and doing what you love to do.

The Final Word

You Can Make It Happen

There are only two mistakes one can make along the road to truth; not going all the way, and not starting.

—BUDDHA

Most of us want to live a life of integrity, which means being true to ourselves. You're an inventor, so creating things, dreaming up ideas and products, and wanting to make a positive difference in the world are all important to you. Now it's time to take the big risk and walk your talk. I can tell you, you will be so much happier—and more in balance with your true self—when you do. Is it scary? You bet! Is it worth it? Absolutely! And remember that people do it all the time.

In fact, many successful people had to overcome staggering odds to "make it." The next time you look at people who are rich and/or famous and think, "Wow, were they ever lucky!" just remember that you don't

know the whole story. Some were abused as kids. Some were in abusive marriages. Some started their businesses out of the trunk of the car they were living in. Some had two or three failed businesses before one made it big. You'd be surprised how many top business leaders struggle with various diagnoses and issues (depression, ADD, ADHD, OCD) and were ridiculed and teased all through school. Others were told by society that they were too old or too young or too differently abled to start something.

But one thing they all had in common was gumption. They applied their smarts and their willpower to their situation—and they rose like the sun. And if they can do it, so can you.

Fear of failure is what keeps so many of us on the ground, working like drones at thankless jobs for bosses we hate just because we're afraid to try something on our own. But—as so many people are finding out—even the most "secure" job can go away in the blink of an eye. The only true job security is your own imagination, your own nerve, your own drive to succeed.

We all have heard that the longest journey begins with a single step. It's time to take it. As you prepare, give some thought to the principles and techniques you learned from this book. Here's a pop quiz to boil it all down into a neat little bouillon cube for you.

THE *IDEA TO INVENTION* FINAL QUIZ

Answer these true/false questions and then look at the key to see how you did.

1. Most products were invented by ordinary people.
   TRUE ☐   FALSE ☐

2. You can turn the solution for an everyday problem into a lucrative invention.
   TRUE ❑   FALSE ❑

3. You need a trust fund to be an inventor: only the wealthy can afford to try.
   TRUE ❑   FALSE ❑   .

4. If you're a naturally quiet person, you'll never succeed.
   TRUE ❑   FALSE ❑

5. Only the people who are totally out for themselves can do well as inventors.
   TRUE ❑   FALSE ❑

6. Curiosity is one of the most important traits to cultivate if you want to be an inventor.
   TRUE ❑   FALSE ❑

7. Don't trust your own instincts: if you're going to be successful, hire lots of experts and believe every word they say.
   TRUE ❑   FALSE ❑

8. Know who you can trust; surround yourself with cheerleaders.
   TRUE ❑   FALSE ❑

9. If someone you know very well tells you you're crazy or you should give up, that person is probably right.
   TRUE ❑   FALSE ❑

10. If someone "in the know" gives you some thoughtful constructive criticism, just ignore it. After all, your idea is perfect!
TRUE ❑   FALSE ❑

11. The best attitude to have when looking for a licensee is "My product is offering you a great opportunity!"
TRUE ❑   FALSE ❑

12. Never toot your own horn. If you've accomplished something worthwhile, just put it out of your mind or you'll get a swelled head.
TRUE ❑   FALSE ❑

13. Everybody has different motivations for wanting to speak out.
TRUE ❑   FALSE ❑

14. When you're telling someone about your product or idea, it's important to be as wordy as possible and to impress her or him with all the big words you know.
TRUE ❑   FALSE ❑

15. If you want to succeed, you have to work, work, work all the time! No breaks! What are you doing sitting there reading this? Get busy!
TRUE ❑   FALSE ❑

16. Use the power of your imagination to visualize best-case, positive scenarios rather than scary, doom-and-gloom ones.
TRUE ❑   FALSE ❑

17. When you're filled with self-doubt, take time to remind yourself of all the things you've managed to accomplish.
TRUE ❑   FALSE ❑

18. When you reach an impasse, it's a sign you should just give up.
     TRUE ❑   FALSE ❑

19. It can be helpful to write a list of all the benefits your idea will offer
     to a customer, or to the world.
     TRUE ❑   FALSE ❑

20. It's always best to pay somebody else a lot of money to take your
     idea to market. Because that person knows better than you do,
     right?
     TRUE ❑   FALSE ❑

21. Every product began as an idea, so it's important to feed your own
     imagination and think creatively, not only "outside the box," but
     without any box at all. What box?
     TRUE ❑   FALSE ❑

22. If you have a good idea, you should immediately hire somebody
     to get you a full-on nonprovisional patent, even though it's
     expensive.
     TRUE ❑   FALSE ❑

23. It's vital to do research online and in stores to see if anything like
     your idea is already out there, to get names of possible licensees, and
     to gather information that could be helpful to you.
     TRUE ❑   FALSE ❑

24. If a company is curious about your idea, share every detail about it
     that you can think of before the company loses interest.
     TRUE ❑   FALSE ❑

25. It can be hugely helpful and informative to make a prototype of your product just to see if it works and what parts you'll need to make the final product.
TRUE ☐   FALSE ☐

26. Any attorney will be a good patent attorney.
TRUE ☐   FALSE ☐

27. A provisional patent application is just as expensive and difficult to obtain as a full (or nonprovisional) patent.
TRUE ☐   FALSE ☐

28. You may not need to worry about paying for a nonprovisional patent if you find a licensee.
TRUE ☐   FALSE ☐

29. Don't bother making cold calls; they're just a waste of time. Send an e-mail instead.
TRUE ☐   FALSE ☐

30. It can help to write a script to use when you're making a cold call so you have an idea of what you want to say.
TRUE ☐   FALSE ☐

31. Trade shows are a big waste of time and money.
TRUE ☐   FALSE ☐

32. You can have a professional-looking table at a trade show without spending a fortune on it; there are lots of corners you can cut.
TRUE ☐   FALSE ☐

33. The term "press kit" refers to those small travel irons you can easily pack in a carry-on, a must if you want to look professional and wrinkle-free.
    TRUE ❑   FALSE ❑

34. If you get a company to license your product, it will do all the work of manufacturing and promoting it and you will get a percentage of the profits.
    TRUE ❑   FALSE ❑

35. If you start your own business, good customer service is key.
    TRUE ❑   FALSE ❑

36. If you're just starting out with a small business, manufacturing your product overseas is cheaper and definitely the way to go, and you can make all the arrangements yourself.
    TRUE ❑   FALSE ❑

37. Once your product is selling well, just sit back and relax! You don't have to give it another thought.
    TRUE ❑   FALSE ❑

38. The Internet is a huge time-sucking sinkhole that offers absolutely nothing to me as an inventor.
    TRUE ❑   FALSE ❑

39. You really need a website if you want to be taken seriously.
    TRUE ❑   FALSE ❑

40. Spending time making fresh entries on your social media sites can lead to more attention for you and your products.

    TRUE ❑   FALSE ❑

41. Only expensive, professionally made videos about products are any good.

    TRUE ❑   FALSE ❑

42. Tweets are online posts of 140 words or less.

    TRUE ❑   FALSE ❑

43. The Internet is one place where you really need to go for the hard sell everywhere and in any way you can think of.

    TRUE ❑   FALSE ❑

44. LinkedIn is like an online chamber of commerce that connects you to millions of professionals around the world.

    TRUE ❑   FALSE ❑

45. Your most important resource as an inventor is *you*: your personality, your interests, your strengths—even your weaknesses.

    TRUE ❑   FALSE ❑

Answer Key

1. **TRUE**—Yes, and if they can do it, so can you.

2. **TRUE**—Absolutely, and in fact it's how many, many products came into being.

3. FALSE—This is *so* false, but the belief is what keeps so many people from giving inventing a try.

4. FALSE—Having a voice doesn't mean being loud and obnoxious! You can be a quiet person but speak with strength so that you'll really get through to others.

5. FALSE—In fact, it is often those who truly want to help others, give to others, and improve things who really succeed.

6. TRUE—Curiosity is what keeps us alert to possibilities.

7. FALSE—While you will most likely need a good accountant, an attorney, and maybe a graphic designer, the most important resource you have is your own instincts.

8. TRUE—Having a healthy support group is very important for anyone, especially for inventors.

9. FALSE—Nope, in fact what they probably are is threatened by you. Avoid the naysayers! Get out the cloves of garlic for such energy-sucking vampires!

10. FALSE—After you get over feeling a little hurt or defensive, look at what was said from a detached place. Maybe the criticism is valuable and can help you improve your idea.

11. TRUE—Rather than feeling like you're begging for attention, keep in mind that your idea could be a gold mine for some lucky company.

12. **FALSE**—Taking time to remind yourself of everything you've accomplished is really important, helping to build your self-confidence.

13. **TRUE**—And it can help to know whether you're more motivated by a desire to teach, inspire, help, or connect.

14. **FALSE**—Brief is better. Keep it as simple and to-the-point as possible; people's attention spans are shortening by the minute.

15. **FALSE**—In fact, you need to take breaks to energize and clear your mind, and to keep your body fit and in shape.

16. **TRUE**—Your mind is powerful. Imagining positive, happy-making futures can release neurochemicals that will make your body feel more relaxed. It's hard to be creative when you're tense.

17. **TRUE**—Some of us even keep a little journal where we jot down all our accomplishments. Then on bad days we can reread them, just as a reminder.

18. **FALSE**—No, no, no! It's just a sign you might need to think about it a different way.

19. **TRUE**—It's good to remind yourself that your idea offers benefits that will be helpful to others, so you won't be tempted to throw in the towel every time you hit a roadblock. Remember all the reasons why the world needs your product!

20. **FALSE**—The world is full of people who will take large chunks of your money to supposedly promote your product to people who will

license it, but chances are you will do a better job yourself—at no cost.

21. TRUE—Your creative imagination is your best ally if you want to be an inventor.

22. FALSE—While you will probably need to protect your idea with a provisional patent application (PPA), you may not need to worry about getting a full-on nonprovisional patent at all, depending on the route you choose to go.

23. TRUE—Research is a fun way to start putting solid ground under the feet of your idea.

24. FALSE—Make sure the company has at least signed a non-disclosure agreement (NDA) first, or that your idea is protected with a PPA or a full patent.

25. TRUE—And it's a lot of fun, besides.

26. FALSE—Not every attorney is a patent attorney. Patent attorneys are a specialized breed with the extra training and schooling needed to be qualified in this area of the law.

27. FALSE—It's much less expensive and less difficult to file a PPA than a nonprovisional patent.

28.   TRUE—While it will still be your responsibility to make sure the details of the patent are accurate, the financial costs may be borne by your licensee.

29. **FALSE**—E-mail lacks the personal touch. Cold calls can be tremen-dously important because they start the process of building personal relationships with potential buyers or licensees.

30. **TRUE**—It can help ease the jitters, too, and practicing with your script can make you sound self-confident and relaxed.

31. **FALSE**—You can make lots of great contacts at a trade show—store buyers, potential licensees, and customers—as well as generate good press and buzz for your idea, and get your product out there in front of the perfect target audience.

32. **TRUE**—You don't have to break the bank to make a good showing at a trade show.

33. **FALSE**—Um, no—a press kit is a packet of promotional materials you put together about your product so reporters covering the trade show can get excited about it.

34. **TRUE**—And it's a route many inventors are choosing to take because it's easier in many ways.

35. **TRUE**—In fact, customer service may be what will make your com-pany stand out from the competition.

36. **FALSE**—Actually, overseas manufacturing is so complicated that it is probably best left to the experts who know how to wade through rivers of paperwork.

37. **FALSE**—Inventors need to be constantly thinking of ways to add to

their product, or vary it, or find another use for it in order to keep it flying off the shelves.

38. FALSE—The Internet is a fantastic tool for any inventor that can help you promote and sell your product easily, quickly, and less expensively.

39. TRUE—Yup, you do. Websites offer people a fast way to find out about you and your products.

40. TRUE—The time it takes to make an entry on Facebook and Twitter or to do a short blog, and then to connect all of these along with a mention of your website, is time well spent and can really pay off.

41. FALSE—You can snag a lot of interest about your ideas with videos made on your phone!

42. FALSE—Tweets are 140 *characters* or less: that's really, really short.

43. FALSE—In fact, online presences that offer interesting or helpful information are far more successful than sites that shout "Buy my product!"

44. TRUE—And it can be a cornucopia of helpful contacts.

45. TRUE—Now get out there and set the world ablaze with your creative, individual, wonderful ideas.

Index

ABOUT THE AUTHOR

A self-professed "ordinary person" and mother of three, Patricia Nolan-Brown has been inventing and marketing problem-solving products for more than 22 years. Among her many inventions is a best-selling car seat mirror, sold internationally, which enables drivers to see infants placed in rear-facing car seats. She has sold tens of millions of products, holds multiple patents and registered trademarks, and is often called "The Mother of Invention."

In addition to being a serial inventor, Nolan-Brown is also a consultant, video-blogger, and motivational speaker for widely diverse groups: from Fortune 500 CEOs to grade-school science-fair hopefuls. She has demystified the invention process for thousands of people and helped them convert their ideas into must-have merchandise.

Her business savvy and warm, humorous style have made Patricia a popular guest on radio shows from Austin to New Zealand. She and her inventions have also been featured in many newspapers and in national magazines and newscasts.

Patricia lives just north of Boston with her husband, three daughters, and her westie, Coconut.

To access additional information, or to book a consultation with Patricia, please visit www.patricianolanbrown.com. You can follow her on Twitter at @pnolanbrown.

*Wishing you
all the very best
ideas and inspirations.*